THE DUST DRAWS ITS FACE ON THE WIND

Praise for *The Dust Draws Its Face on the Wind*

'When "the factory of poetry" shuts down, the natural spring of poetry becomes audible—Avinash Shrestha's voice is that spring. Building upon conventions of the lyric and of universal symbols and fables and then either toppling them or surpassing them to claim his own distinct poetic space, Shrestha's vision taps into the consciousness of the world, assimilating and transcending cultures. Rohan Chhetri's translations flow smoothly and succeed in catching the syntactic patterns of Nepali, helping us become friends with one of Nepal's most moving and significant poetic voices.'

—Mani Rao

'The poems [in *The Dust Draws Its Face on the Wind*] sing with chimerical music and demonstrate Shrestha's singular use of language that blends Hindu liturgical elements and Vedic cosmology, Sanskrit-rooted high diction and Nepali vernacular, together with a tender branch of surrealism within postmodern aesthetics. Poet and emerging translator Rohan Chhetri's work as translator begins with the well-considered decision to translate these exquisite, "wild by design" poems by Shrestha, and ends with a body of brilliant, culturally complex poems that have roots across the South Asian diaspora.'

—PEN/Heim Translation Fund Grants, Judges Citation
(Kareem James Abu-Zeid, Peter Constantine, Karen Emmerich,
Nicholas Glastonbury, Elisabeth Jaquette, Tess Lewis,
Aditi Machado, Sawako Nakayasu, Wanda Phipps,
Jeremy Tiang, Lara Vergnaud, and Jeffrey Zuckerman)

THE DUST DRAWS ITS FACE ON THE WIND

SELECTED POEMS

AVINASH SHRESTHA

TRANSLATED FROM THE NEPALI BY
ROHAN CHHETRI

HARPERPERENNIAL
An Imprint of HarperCollins *Publishers*

First published in English in India by Harper Perennial 2024
An imprint of HarperCollins *Publishers*
4th Floor, Tower A, Building No. 10, DLF Cyber City,
DLF Phase II, Gurugram, Haryana – 122002
www.harpercollins.co.in

2 4 6 8 10 9 7 5 3 1

P-ISBN: 978-93-6213-356-4
E-ISBN: 978-93-6213-122-5

Typeset in 11.5/16 EB Garamond at
HarperCollins *Publishers* India

Printed and bound at
Thomson Press (India) Ltd

Contents

'Descend the Ineffable into a Syllable'

Translating Avinash Shrestha

I first started translating Avinash Shrestha's poetry in an introductory translation class at Syracuse University in 2018. The year before, I had come across a small archival feature on him online from a 2003 issue of *Nepali Times,* with two of his poems translated by the writer Manjushree Thapa, who had noted that his work was 'some of the most interior, emotionally charged poetry being written today by any male poet'. Through some sources, I procured an old copy of *Anubhuti Yatrama* (On a Journey through Intimations), his third book published in 1990, and began reading. Even though I'd been writing poetry in English for years, I hadn't kept up with reading much Nepali contemporary poetry since the poets I'd read in school. However, somewhere in the back of my head, I had been searching for a project I could (and *should*) translate. As an Indian–Nepali Anglophone poet, I had, more than once, the charge of not writing in Nepali levelled at me. I thought translating Nepali poetry could assuage that complaint. The field was open. I soon realized I had no serious models. Beyond a few genuine but scattered efforts in anthologies and academic essays—including the very important archival work of Michael Hutt, a lifelong scholar of Nepali literature—no concerted effort had been made to translate a full-length collection by a contemporary Nepali poet, much less a retrospective on a poet's selected works, and bring it to a larger anglophone audience. The few Nepali poets I had read since my schooling in Kalimpong, West Bengal, I thought, were still plagued by righteous social critiques that seemed dated.

I was proved wrong. I simply hadn't read enough. I found Shrestha's elliptical poems in *Anubhuti Yatrama* challenging and interesting linguistically, and their uncanny use of image and unpredictable metaphors were unlike anything I'd read in Nepali. I had the first inkling of finally finding Nepali poems that, in translating into English, would take my own language elsewhere. There was an undercurrent in Shrestha's poetry that was unruly, which I felt had its lineage somewhere else, in some other modernism or tradition of world poetry. In many of his poems, Shrestha seems to be consciously playing with vestiges of high Sanskritized 'tatsam' diction drawn from Assamese and Bengali poetry in India, which he uses to subvert and disrupt how Nepali poetry is traditionally expected to sound. He achieves this by his use of changing registers, alternating and mixing 'high' Sanskritized and 'low' folk diction, and also by using images and concepts from the Hindu liturgical tradition and Vedic cosmology, and finally, by pushing these against a surrealist, 'deep image' aesthetic that is modernist in impulse. In the best of Shrestha's poems, I have found the quality of all good poetry—the encapsulation of the cosmic scope of the universe, the distillation of humanity's history and experience, its suffering and elation, its revelation and collective triumph, in a single image or a line or a turn of phrase.

In the preface to *Anubhuti Yatrama*, Avinash Shrestha writes,

> I often feel this desire again and again to venture outside of language, but by never actually crossing the boundary of language. I know that this is a difficult task. But those truths that are far outside of language, you cannot harness them in a poem by trudging through the same old tracks; and therefore I experiment.

He sums up his aesthetic project as a kind of grappling with this fugal sensibility, this poetic predisposition to wander 'outside of language' to find something that must ultimately be reined within language. He further explains his reverence for formal tradition, but at the same time his belief in the provisionality of form that is malleable to the shape of what he *wrestles* into utterance. Thus, he writes, he believes in the living, dynamic nature of formal tradition instead of a dogmatic one. He does this by working in a mode pitched towards a repurposing of tradition and a home-grown surrealism. Finally, he talks of this mode as his way of bypassing *paddhatigrastata,* or 'mannerism', as he writes in parentheses. This idea first appears in the poem 'Aside', from the collection *Parewa: Seto Kala* (Pigeons: White, Black):

> I do not desire to live
> far from meaning   whether meaning stirs
> outside of words—I'm trying
> to find   let me seek
>
> Let me dig, exhale
>   breathbloom
> the many subterranean rooms of anguish
> allow me to search without speech
> some wordless intimation

Although published as his second book in 1984, *Parewa: Seto Kala* was technically his first collection. The copies were destroyed before they were distributed, in a press raid in Benares in 1977. Avinash was around twenty-two years old then.

Shrestha's inclusion of the English word 'mannerism' in parentheses along with the Nepali/Sanskrit equivalent *paddhatigrastata* in the preface to *Anubhuti Yatrama* is worth noting. The word comes from the Sanskrit *paddhati* meaning 'way, mode, method, system' and *grasta* meaning 'affectation, possession, seized', with *ta* as a noun suffix. Mannerism, a term borrowed from art history, was used to describe a highly affected literary style in the early seventeenth century. Hence, in the evolution of stylistic periods, Shrestha consciously places his work beyond what he perceives as 'mannerism' in Nepali poetry of the mid-twentieth century. This led me to read his work within the framework of an emerging 'baroque' impulse, which evolves from the culmination and full expression of high mannerism in seventeenth-century art. Thus, the ingenuity of form and high rhetoric of social and moral critiques in Nepali poetry break away towards more eccentric themes and a flamboyant style turned inward in Shrestha's poetry.

However, his artistic lineage wasn't as simple as I'd imagined. By his own admission, when Shrestha moved to Nepal as a postgraduate student in 1984, he wasn't well versed with the contemporary poets in Nepal. His literary sensibility had been nourished instead by the Assamese, Bengali, Hindi and Urdu contemporary literary traditions. But he was also reading, by the late 70s and 80s, world poetry ranging from the French symbolist poets to the Spanish surrealist poet Federico García Lorca, the Chilean poet Pablo Neruda and the Italian poet Salvatore Quasimodo, to American poets from Walt Whitman to Allen Ginsberg. While doing a Bachelor of Science degree in Guwahati, Assam in 1973–75, Shrestha spent time with classmates who were painters, poets and theatre actors. He was soon made a co-opted member of the

Guwahati Artists' Guild, a meeting place for many prominent Assamese writers, artists and actors of the time. Watching these artists work closely, he saw in the language of visual arts the use of juxtaposition—real-world objects like a cigarette packet became a part of the canvas, breaking a two-dimensional painting. In the early 1980s, at the height of the Assam Movement, 'collage' became a revolutionary idiom for the Nepali poets in Assam, and Avinash Shrestha spearheaded this collage movement in Nepali poetry. The Cuban Revolution and the impossible guerrilla wars led by Che Guevara and Fidel Castro further informed the revolutionary impulse of artists and poets at the time. Furthermore, the post-Independence ecological–social movements in India, like the Chipko Movement and the Narmada Bachao Andolan, provided an ecocritical framework to Shrestha's poetry. The poems written under the influence of this era were collected in *Samvedna, O Samvedna!* (Intimations, Oh Intimations!, 1981), his first published collection. The title poem from the book was awarded the prestigious Ratnashree Swarna Padak in Nepal. A prize conferred by the royal palace and named after the queen, it was judged by the eminent poet Siddhicharan Shrestha and prominent critic Dr Vasudev Tripathi, suddenly launching Shrestha into the Nepali literary scene in Kathmandu. On the invitation of Dr Tripathi at Tribhuvan University, Avinash Shrestha came to pursue a postgraduate degree in Kathmandu in 1984 on a scholarship. During his time at the university, Shrestha's work started gaining more serious recognition from eminent Nepali poets like Vijay Malla, Bhupi Sherchan, Krishna Bhakta Shrestha and Basu Shashi. Eight of his poems, including 'Spell', were published in the Royal Nepal Academy's magazine, *Kavita*. Similarly, Parijat (Bishnu

Kumari Waiba), a prominent Marxist-feminist poet, published 'Of Some Unidentified Village, Nayantara Barua' in *Utsah*, a magazine she was editing in 1987.

The 1960s had been an interesting period in Nepali poetry. A long turbulent decade after the revolution of 1950–51 that overthrew the Rana regime, the 60s marked a period of a new political consciousness in Nepal. Plagued by authoritarianism and suppression of freedom of expression and knowledge, where writers could be jailed for starting a library, the Rana era (1846–1951) had seen many prominent writers of the previous generation flee to Patna, Calcutta, Benares and Lucknow for education and to avoid censorship. The ones who stayed, like Gopalprasad Rimal, Kedar Man Vyathit and Siddhicharan Shrestha, were frequently jailed for their explicitly revolutionary poems. After years of factional strife and multiple elections, in 1957 a democratic government was formed under the prime ministership of B.P. Koirala. On 15 December 1960, King Mahendra dismissed this democratic government, imprisoning many of the key players of the erstwhile ruling party and created his own one-party Panchayat government with the king as the head of state. The next thirty years of the Panchayat regime saw heightened censorship, curtailing of press freedom and freedom of speech. Writers and poets continued to be imprisoned for any contrarian expression against the new government. It was under these circumstances that a new poetry emerged in the 1960s to escape censorship. Poets like Mohan Koirala, Krishna Bhakta Shrestha, Dwarika Shrestha, Bhuwan Dhungana and Madan Regmi were the forerunners of this new Prayogvadi Kavita movement, using absurdism and experimentalism to fly under the radar of the Panchayat dictatorship. These poets further branched into other subversive poetry camps like the Boot Polish movement and the Amlekh movement. *Rooprekha*, one of the most prominent Nepali literary magazines of the 60s, served as a conduit for this new experimental poetry. Alongside this, in response to the abstruse experimentalism came the Saral Kavita movement, marked by simplicity, irony, and the direct expression of protest poetry helmed by poets like Bhupi Sherchan, Parijat, Basu Shashi, Mohan Hemangshu Thapa, Jasraj Kirati and Upendra Shrestha. Around the same time, poets like Raamesh, Rayn, Neenu, Manjul and, later, Parijat, started the dissident movement in poetry and music called Ralpha against the rule of the Panchayat government. Begun initially as an apolitical aesthetic movement, it was later influenced by left-front politics, French existential philosophy, surrealism and the Cuban Revolution. Another key literary movement, Tesro Ayam (The Third Dimension), took shape during the same time that redefined Nepali modernism. Begun from Darjeeling, India, by writers Indra Bahadur Rai, Bairagi Kainla and Ishwar Ballav, it was heavily influenced by the Anglo-American modernism of Pound and Eliot, the French avant-garde and cubism, the corpus of folk literature and mythology, as well as psychoanalysis. The Tesro Ayam movement urged writers to eschew sentimentalism and access a 'third' dimension that could add a new depth and perception to Nepali literature. It was a clear rejection of the anti-intellectualism and sentimentalism of the earlier literature.

Around 1973, a middle path emerged called 'Samasamayik Kavita Dhara', a subversive 'contemporary' poetry movement marked by clarity of image and symbolism. This poetry spoke of the Nepali underclass and protested the ruling government obliquely without overt sloganeering. In the 80s, the critics in Nepal placed Avinash Shrestha's poetry somewhere between this new Samasamayik poetry movement and the experimentalism of the Prayogvadi poets of the 60s. It was against this groundwork of a new direction in the sensibility of Nepali poetry laid by the poets before him that Avinash Shrestha's poetry appeared in the late 70s and 80s in Nepal. It was undoubtedly received with a degree of uncertainty. Michael Hutt in his book *Himalayan Voices* published in 1991 introduced him as 'unique among the younger generation of Nepali poets', further writing that 'his work has caused a stir in Kathmandu literary circles ... [His] poems are heavy with mystical symbolism; their beauty is indisputable, but their interpretation is the subject of vigorous debate'. By 1984–85, Shrestha, devoid of political affiliations, had turned towards ecological and environmental concerns in his poetry.

In 1987, after finishing his postgraduate degree, Shrestha decided to go back to India. After searching for a job unsuccessfully for the next three years across Sikkim, Assam and West Bengal, in 1990, he returned to Kathmandu for good and began writing for TV and feature films for the Nepali film industry. He also began serving as the executive editor at the Royal Nepal Academy in the same year. The influences of the last decade metabolized in his next book, *Anubhuti Yatrama*, with its arcane imagery and surrealist juxtapositions in poems like 'Inattention' and 'Spell', and forceful and revolutionary rhythms in poems like 'Of Some Unidentified Village, Nayantara Barua', which directly addresses the Nellie Massacre of 1983, a dark chapter of the Assam Movement. Shrestha's first book to be published in Nepal, *Anubhuti Yatrama*, was unlike any poetry being written around that time in Nepal. His detractors found his imagery too abstruse, his nonconformity to linearity, his opacity and resistance to interpretation too foreign. The Nepali literary culture was divided along party lines and Shrestha's nonpartisan stance in Nepali politics alienated him further.

In a way, Shrestha was a unique case of a 'double interloper' in Nepali poetry. He had forged a quintessentially modern Nepali diction and imagery. Along with this, he had infused a distinctly Sanskrit-heavy inflorescence—drawn from the Assamese, Urdu, Hindi and Bengali poetry of India—into the idiom of Nepali poetry that was, at the time, mired in social critiques. Shrestha's use of Sanskritized Nepali and liturgical lexicon beside common spoken Nepali with an often conscious smattering of English words, his juxtaposition of the sacred and the profane, and his changing registers from high eloquence to vulgarity at once brought the 'language of the gods' to the streets and the hearth, and in turn elevated the vernacular of a still-globalizing third world in the equalizing and democratic space of the poem. *Anubhuti Yatrama* resuscitated Nepali poetry to the history and condition of its own utterance, making itself aware of its own rhizomatic linguistic relations. This new poetry was syncretic, surrealistic, and a culmination of his wide-ranging poetic sensibilities. Shrestha's most recent full-length collection, *Karodoun Suryaharuko Andhakar* (Darkness of a Million Suns, 2003), intersects his distinct brand of surrealism perfected in his first three books with themes of ecology and climate justice that pervade his entire oeuvre, reflecting the ecological turn his poetry took in the mid-1980s.

The selection of the poems in this edition was primarily made by me—through trial and error as I wrestled with the translations over the years—with some suggestions from Shrestha whose choices were sometimes at odds with my own. I was thinking of the translated text as a creative act in and of itself, a radical 'afterlife' of the original poem. This idea is contrary to the prevalent idea of translation as the transference of some 'invariant' from the original source language into the target language. I don't think it is helpful to think of the translation of poetry in these merely functional terms, especially with the vast difference in the two languages at hand. Moreover, I believe each language maps and inhabits too particular and concrete a reality of the world, a unity of meaning and sound, to allow for any such neat transference of expressions and sensibilities from one language to another. Yet, it would be a stretch to say my translations are 'free' in the way translations are described as 'free' or 'faithful'. I understand that having a bilingual edition naturally invites heightened comparison and scrutiny through that old metric of 'fidelity'. But the virtue of precision, which is the very thing put to the test in translation, was not my primary rubric for these translations. Instead, I was concerned with how I could allow the cadence and syntactic peculiarities of Nepali to infiltrate and contaminate the English, all in service of the unusual syntactic 'order of disclosure' and imagistic strangeness that is inherent in Shrestha's poems. In the end, my work was that of a negotiator, to facilitate and contain this contentious meeting of the two languages and cultures in the translated text. This allowed me to slide across the scale of 'fidelity' in each poem, line, stanza, on a case-by-case basis, dependant on what the translated poem demanded.

Ultimately, this is my version of Avinash Shrestha's poems, down to the curation, with its various elisions, interpretations and critical frameworks that I have applied within the limitations of my own knowledge and interests. I do not intend at all for this to be the definitive version of Shrestha in English; I hope future translators will take on Shrestha's work, particularly the poems that I have left behind in the Nepali. I, admittedly, chose poems that challenged me in translation, and in this endeavour have neglected the longer, more narrative poems—poems of a clearer, sometimes poignant, vein—that I realized were being flattened by my hand when rendered in English. For the most part, I favoured the more interior, surrealistic and lyric poems. I chose poems that were striving to 'Descend / the ineffable / into a syllable', because through translating these I could strive to replicate the very 'process' of indeterminacy that seemed to be at work in the writing of these poems. In the best of these poems, I had to first locate this 'ineffable' and follow through the indeterminacy of its 'descent' into English, thus in a small way rerouting the reader to that original impulse of the Nepali poem. My hope is that I have invented *one* discernible, recognizable voice in the translation of these poems. A voice that, although moves distinctly, metamorphosing through the stylistic evolution of Shrestha's poetry, ultimately remains its own entity. A 'collaborative' voice, if you will, that has facilitated this meeting, yet neither claiming to be the author's nor the translator's, but a third—perhaps the fugal Other that appears in Shrestha's poems. I hope future translators working on his poems will uncover many more such voices.

—Rohan Chhetri

June 2024, Houston

THE DUST DRAWS ITS FACE ON THE WIND

कवि हुनु

दुहुनु
ईथरबाट
सन्नाटाको सङ्गीत ।

बन्नु
शून्यबाट
असङ्ख्य ।

थाप्नु
शब्दमा
निःशब्द ।

थप्नु
सृष्टिमा
सुगन्ध ।

उमार्नु
माटोमा
ब्रह्माण्ड ।

ओराल्नु
अविदितलाई
अक्षरमा ।

Poet's Work

Milk
from the firmament
music of dead silence.

Become
innumerable
from nought.

Receive
in words
what is wordless.

Add
redolence
to creation.

Sprout
from the soil
a cosmos.

Descend
the ineffable
into a syllable.

From *Karodoun Suryaharuko Andhakar* (Darkness of a Million Suns), 2003

the air
you have polluted you will breathe
the waters
you have poisoned you will drink
when you come again and you will come again

—Lucille Clifton, 'the message from The Ones
(received in the late 70s)'

सापेक्ष

चट्टानहरू सुन्दर छन्
फूलहरूभन्दा पनि सुन्दर छन्

काँडाहरू उदास छन्
रङ्गहरूभन्दा पनि उदास छन्

मन उड्दै छ माथि-माथि
पुतलीहरूभन्दा, चराहरूभन्दा कता हो कता माथि

उमेर बग्दै छ
पग्लेको सुन बग्दै छ

भ्रमले भ्रमलाई, भ्रमलाई फेरि भ्रमले छोपेको छ
अँध्यारोले रातलाई, रातलाई फेरि अँध्यारोले छोपेझैं ।

Relative

The cliffs are beautiful
Even more beautiful than flowers

The thorns are sorrowful
Even more sorrowful than colours

The heart drifts high, high above
Even higher than the butterflies, the birds

Age flows
Molten gold flows

Illusion enfolds illusion, in turn hidden by another illusion
Like night enfolds darkness, and darkness hides by night

कायाकल्प

नदीलाई अँगालो मारेर निर्धक्क निदाउँछु
र ब्युँझँदा निस्सीम समुद्र बनेको हुन्छु

रातभरि बिपनामा झुसिल्कीराको जुनीमा घस्रिरहेको थिएँ
अहिले मध्यदिनको सपनामा रङ्गीन पुतलीमा फेरिएर उडिरहेछु

म मैमत्त, परपीडक तर दीर्घायु काँडा थिएँ हिजोसम्मन्
कुन्नि कुन निष्ठुरीले झारिदिएछ मलाई – फूलको क्षणिक कायामा

'प्वाँख' म जथाभावी उडिरहेको हुन्छु – बतासको बुई चढेर
अनि चरा बन्ने आदिम आकाङ्क्षा हुर्काइरहेको हुन्छु आत्माभित्र

म मात्र 'बीउ' छु आज – मलाई राम्ररी थाहा छ
भोलि 'ईश्वर' मैबाट टुसाउनेछ हेरिराख ।

Metamorphosis

Embracing the river I fall asleep unafraid
& when I wake I become the boundless sea

All night I crawled awake in the lifespan of a caterpillar
In the afternoon dream I've transformed into a butterfly in bright air

I was arrogant, cruel but an imperishable thorn until yesterday
Someone heartless has dropped me—in the flower's brief body

A feather I drift wherever—piggybacking on the wind
In my soul I nurse a primitive desire to be a bird

I'm only a seed today—I know
Tomorrow, you watch, God will sprout from me

लालसा

मनभित्रको एकलासमा
निःशब्द छ
नीलो अन्धकार छ
र छ तिम्रो आभास ।

तिमी : जहाँसम्म पुग्न
एक जन्मले पुग्दैन मलाई ।

तिमीसम्म पुग्ने सृजन-यात्राको
म यात्री
तर बाटाहरू कति छन् भने
म तिनलाई रोज्नमै अलमलिएको छु ।

हरेक बाटोले मलाई
तिमीसम्म पुऱ्याउने दावा गर्छ
बाटाहरू बाटाहरू बनेर होइन
बाटाहरू स्वयम् तिम्रो अभिनय गर्दै
तिमीसम्म पुग्ने बाटो छेकेर
उभिएका छन् मेरो अघिल्तिर ।

र पछिल्तिर...
मेरो पछिल्तिर छ
मैले मर्दै आएको क्रमिक मृत्यु
मृत्युलाई पछि हुत्याउँदै म
क्रमशः अगाडि गुडिरहेको छु
जीवनको लिकमा
गन्तव्यमा तिमी भेटिने लालसा लिई ।

Greed

Deep in the heart's remoteness
there is quiet
In the blue darkness there is
an apparition of you

You—to arrive at the edge of you
my one birth will not do

In the creation-odyssey of arriving towards you
I'm a pilgrim
But there are so many roads
Having to choose bewilders me

Each road promises
it will lead me to you
And the roads—they speak not as themselves
the roads impersonate you
Standing in front of me
in the way of my path to you

Behind me—
There are
the many increments of my serial deaths
Shoving each death behind
I hurtle on
                along the laddered track
                greedy that at the destination I might find you

श्रम-गीत

कसैले थाहा नपाउने गरी
आँखामा हराएको छ एउटा महानगर

कसैले चाल नपाउने गरी
छातीमा खनिएको छ एउटा पोखरी

कसैले बुझ्नै नसक्ने गरी
ओठमा बिलाएको छ एउटा उपत्यका

कसैले पढ्नै नभ्याउने लिपिमा
हत्केलामा कुँदिएका छन् कविता

आँखामा छ प्रेमको महानगर
छातीमा घृणाको पोखरी
ओठमा तिम्रै – गीतैगीतको उपत्यका
अनि हत्केलामा श्रमका ठेला-गिर्खाका
शब्दहरूले कुँदिएका कविता

म
पूर्ण हुन चाहन्छु
मान्छेको चोलामा
तिम्रो प्रेमलाई
र
श्रमलाई
श्रद्धा गर्दै... ।

Labour-Song

Undiscovered by anyone
there is a city lost in the eyes

Hidden from everyone
a pond dug in the chest

Inscrutable to all
a valley vanishes in the lips

In an illegible hand
a poem is scrawled across the palm

In the eyes a city of love
In the chest a pond of hatred
In the lips—valley of your myriad songs
& across the palm a poem scrawled
from the hard labour of words pulled in a cart

I
want to be whole
in a human form
in devotion
to your love
and to labour

पानी

कार्बनको कोलाहलभित्र
कतै पनि छैन – पानी

धूवाँको धसिङ्गरे अन्धकारभित्र
कहीं पनि हुँदैन – पानी

धूलोको धूसर फोहोरभित्र
कतै पनि पाइँदैन – पानी

बालुवाको बबन्डर निफनेर
कहीं पनि भेटिँदैन – पानी

माटोलाई मथेर मदानीले
हातलागी होला र – पानी ?

ढुङ्गालाई घोटेर ढुङ्गामा
कहाँ रसाएको छ – पानी ?

अम्लको आहाल प्रशोधन गर्दा
बरु बन्ला कि केही थोपा – पानी ।

अब त
मान्छेमै निहित
अग्नि
आकाश
माटो
अनि

Water

Inside the clamour of carbon
nowhere there is—water

Inside the smoke's wintergreen dark
there will not be any—water

Inside the grey cloud of dust
you will not find—water

Winnowing the tumult of sand
you will not suddenly discover—water

If you churn the brown earth with a stick
will you then find—water?

Rubbing two stones together
who has divined—water?

If you distil the murky pond
maybe there'll be a few drops—of water

Now what is retained
in man:
fire
sky
earth
vitality

प्राणतत्त्व
विसर्जन गरी
बाँकी बचेको 'जल' – जोगाउनुपर्छ।

यही जल नै अमर आत्मा हो शरीरको
यही आत्मज-अम्बुज
            जीवन-जल
            पीयूष-रस-पानी
आगामी पुस्ताका निम्ति
            अपार अमृत बन्नेछ – निःसन्देह।

must be cast off
to shore what is left
of water

Body's infinite essence
Born from itself
                    life-sap
                    elixir
For the ones to come in the future
                    nectar inexhaustible water

जाडोको रात

निद्रा
पकेटमा
हात
घुसारेर
पर
उभिएको
छ
चुपचाप ।

फुटपाथमा
कठ्याङ्ग्रिँदै
कामिरहेको
नाङ्गो
देहमा
ब्युँझिरहेको
छ
एक्लो
उदास
जाडोको
रात ।

Winter Night

Sleep
with hands
in its pockets
stands
at
a distance
in
silence

On the footpath
across
a bare
shivering
body
lies
awake
a lonely
sorrowful
winter's
night

पञ्चमहाभूत : एउटा पर्यावरण कविता

चराहरू आकाशतिर उडे
र आकाश भए

वायु-वेगमा कुदिहिँड्ने वन्यजन्तुहरू
वायु भए

मान्छेहरू माटामा लडीबुडी गरिरहे
र माटो नै भए

माछाहरू पानीमा सलबलाइरहे
र पानी नै भए

बिचरा रुखहरू व्यर्थमा सल्काइए, डढाइए
र आगो भए

तर
चरा
वन्यजन्तु
मान्छे
माछा
र रूखका असल आत्माहरू
डढ्न सकेनन् र तेज भए
अनि तिनैबाट बन्यो सूर्यको उज्यालो
नक्षत्रहरूको नीलो झिलमिल रचियो

Song of the Five Elements

The birds flew towards the sky
and became sky

Wild beasts that ran with the speed of wind
became wind itself

Humans rolled over in dirt
and became earth

The fish darted restlessly in water
and became water

The poor trees set to flames for nothing, cindered
and became fire

But
the true souls
of
birds
beasts
humans
fish
and trees
couldn't be burnt so they burnished
and from them was forged the sun's great flare
the constellations' blue flash

तर
कवि – न चरा बन्न तयार थियो
          न माछा बन्न
          न मान्छे बन्न तयार थियो
          न माटो बन्न

त्यसैले
कवि – सुस्केरा बन्यो
          संवेदना बन्यो
          अक्षर बन्यो ।

But

the poet— neither ready to be bird

nor fish

neither ready to be human

nor dirt

Became— a sigh

an intimation

a cipher

अश्व-राग

घोडा जस्तै कुदिरहेछन् दिनहरू
समयको सडकमा ।

कालो घोडा जस्तो रात हिनहिनाउँछ
चन्द्रमुखी चन्द्रमातिर हेरेर ।

एउटा लयमा प्रस्ट बाँधिएको मांसलता
घोडाको ऐश्वर्य हो
र मुखमा घरी-घरी कस्सिन आइपुग्ने लगाम
घोडाको घोर विवशता ......

फेरि पनि
धुकधुकी जस्ता कोमल आफ्ना यालहरूमाथि
घोडालाई
प्रचण्ड गर्व छ ।

यात्रा जोसुकैको किन नहोस्
हिँड्ने आफ्नो आदिम क्षमतालाई
पौरख ठान्छ
र मक्ख पर्छ
घोडा ।

झर्को नमानी
सधैं अरूलाई सयौं कोस बोक्छ
आफूलाई बोक्दा दुई पाइलामै थाक्छ
घोडा ।

Equine-Raga

Like horses the days gallop
on the road of time

Like a black horse the night whinnies
        at the full moon

Its muscles braided in sinuous waves—
the horse's riches
And the bridle that tugs
at its mouth—the horse's anguish

Even so,
the horse's fierce pride
in its mane
softer than a heartbeat

No matter whose journey it is
in its primal ability to gallop
the horse beams
with vigour

Without protest
it carries men for hundreds of miles
yet carrying itself
the horse is exhausted by a trot

सधैं भ्रम भइरहन्छ घोडालाई
कलम जस्तो कठोर ऊसित लिङ्ग छ
मैथुन-विह्वल हुन ऊ फुक्का ठान्छ आफूलाई
सिर्जना गर्न स्वाधीन ठान्छ ऊ आफैलाई

ऊ
भन्ठान्छ –
जन्मन्छन् उसका उन्मत्त शुक्रकीटहरूबाट
असङ्ख्य अक्षरका घोडाहरू ।

घोडाजस्तै कुदिरहेछन् रातहरू
समयको सडकमा ।

Every day the horse nurses an illusion:
it possesses a phallus hard as a pen
To be delirious in coitus it is free
To create in its own image it is unbound

It
believes—
from my swarm of intoxicated sperm
will spring forth innumerable horses

Like horses the nights gallop
on the road of time

जङ्गल : एउटा सलिलक्की

जङ्गललाई मरूभूमितिर लखेट्दै
जङ्गलको अमरताको गीत गाइरहेछु म

जङ्गलसँगै जानेछ सौन्दर्य
रूखसँगसँगै बिदा हुनेछ रूप
शृङ्गार चराहरूसितै उड्नेछ
विदीर्ण हुनेछ नदीसँगसँगै वैभव

उराठिनेछ ठिटो दिन
यौवनका पुतलीहरू वरिपरि नउड्दा
फूलहरू नदेख्दा विचलित हुनेछन् सम्भ्रान्त ऋतुहरू
सुगन्धका सुनकेसरी मैयाँहरूलाई कठै !
हरेर लैजानेछन् दुर्गन्धका दुर्मुख दानवहरूले

बिलखबन्दमा पर्नेछ बतास
पातहरूसित हातेमालो हराउँदा
विषादमा डुब्नेछ जून
खोला र जङ्गलसित लुकामारी बिलाउँदा
निसास्सिनेछ रात
रूखहरूसँग निर्धक्क निदाउन नपाउँदा

लहडी घामले सूर्यको प्रशंसामा
युगौंदेखि गाउँदै आएको न्यानो गीत
एक दिन अलप हुनेछ

Jungle: A Soliloquy

Chasing the jungle to the desert
I sing of the jungle's immortality

With the jungle shall escape all beauty
With the trees shall leave all form
All adornment disappear with the birds
All splendour cleave with the river

Sorrow will loom on the tender day
when the young butterflies no longer swarm the hills
The flowers' vanishing will baffle seasons
The gold-haired nymphs of fragrance
seized by the foul-mouthed demons of reek

The wind will discombobulate
without the leaves' fingers to clasp on to
The moon will drown in desolation
without the hide-and-seek with the rivers, the jungles
The night will asphyxiate
without the trees' arms to fall asleep on

The bright rays shouting the sun's warm praisesong
since the beginning
will one day fall silent

र

अमृतका सरस तालहरू
तिर्खैतिर्खाको बालुवामा फेरिनेछन्
अनि जीवनको कोमल निरन्तरता
अनुवाद हुँदै जानेछ सुस्त-सुस्त
विषाक्त फ्यान्टेसीहरूमा
याब्सट्र्याक्ट खित्काहरूमा
अमूर्त क्रन्दनहरूमा

मान्छे
माटो बन्नेछ
माटो बन्नेछ
निर्जन ।

जङ्गललाई मरूभूमितिर मुन्टचाउँदै
'रूखहरू दीर्घायु होऊन्' भन्ने
मक्किएको मन्त्र
भटचाइरहेछु
म

And
the clear lakes of nectar
will turn to dunes of great thirst
Then life's gentle passage
will have transformed little by little
        into a noxious reverie
        into an abstract fit of laughter
        into an intangible lament

Man
will turn to soil
soil will turn to
desert

Hounding the jungle to the desert
I'm incanting
a rotting spell:
'May the trees forever live'

एकालाप

आशङ्काको चिसो आँखा
हेरिरहन्छ टोलाएर – दिनलाई
अनि मलाई ।

छुरी जस्तो धारिलो डर
सिरानीमुनि घुसार्छु
र निर्धक्क निदाउने उपक्रम गर्छु ।

रात
बोक्सी झैं
झाँक्रो फिँजारी पस्छे
र फिँजिँदै जान्छे –
मेरो अवचेतनमा ।

बजेको सुनिन थाल्छ
रगतमा मेरो
दुःखको आदिम नगरा ।

कौतूहलको जङ्गलबाट निस्केर
एउटा खतरनाक ब्वाँसो
मभित्रको कामुकताको इनारमा
हाम फाल्छ
र कहराइरहन्छ रातभर
निद्रा बिथोल्दै ।

Monologue

Cold eye of doubt
gazes— at the day
at me

I've tucked under my pillow
a bright dagger of fear
and commenced the sleep of the unafraid

Night:
enters like a witch
scattering her matted locks,
diffusing deeper—
in my subconscious

Then begins to ring
in my blood
a primitive drum of sorrow

Out of the woods of curiosity
emerges a ravening
wolf that leaps into the well
of my lust
and howls all night
sleep-poisoning

नीलो चन्द्रमा – किंवदन्तीको
हल्लिरहन्छ
मयूरपङ्खी कामनाको रात जस्तो
गाढा मातको तलाउमा ।

ब्युँतन्छन्
थुप्रै-थुप्रै भऱ्याङ्हरू
एकालापका ।

एक
एक
खुड्किलोमा
भऱ्याङको

एक
एक
पहेंलो गुलाफ ।

पहेंलिएका दिनहरू –
बिछोडका
कुन्नि कसले
छापेर गएछ आज
स्मृतिका
उदास
पानाहरूमा ।

On delirium's lake
a blue rumoured moon
shivers iridescent
like a peacock-feathered night of desire

Then awaken
the many stairs
of the monologue

For
each
tread
of
the stairs

a
yellow
rose.

Yellowed days—
of estrangement
Who knows
whose imprints are these
on the
sorrow-sheets
of memory

कुइरो लागेको पहाडबाट झर्दै गर्दा

कविताको कारखाना बन्द गरेर
कुइरोको गाउँतिर ओर्लिरहेछु ।

जथाभाबी हाँसिरहने खैरा-पहेँला पातहरू
सामसुम्म थिए बाटाभरि
बाटाभरि किन हो किन अहिले
सुसेल्न मन लागेन ।
हावा जस्तै हजारतिरबाट
आफै ओइरिरहने – कता-कताका गीतहरू
कति-कति कन्दा पनि
सम्झन सकिनँ
आज ।

माथि-माथि थिएँ –
कहाँ हो कहाँ माथि
भावुक संसारमा आफू ।
तल-तल थिए साना-साना
निर्धन-निर्दोष घरहरू
यथार्थका
अनि
गाई-भैंसी, भेडा-बाख्रा, घोडा-खच्चडजस्ता
जस्ता बनिसकेका मान्छे ।

तैपनि
भोको सन्तोकलाई च्यापेर
आत्मीय मित्रलाई झैं
हिँडिरहें
खडेरी परेको मौसमतिर ।

On Descending a Fog-Rimmed Mountain

Shutting the factory of poetry
I'm descending towards the village of fog

The scattered laughter of yellow-brown leaves
muted along the trail
                    along the trail for some reason
                    I couldn't bring myself to whistle

Like wind blowing from a thousand directions
unbidden—   fragmented music
                    I couldn't remember the words for
                    hard as I tried

I was high, high above—
Who knows how high
               in a sentimental world
Down, down below were tiny
poor, unsullied houses
               of reality
               and like the
cows and buffalos, sheep and lambs, horses and mules
               were people down there

Clutching a hungry contentment
close like a soul-companion
               I walked
               towards the drought-ridden weather

हिनहिनाइरहेथ्यो भित्रको कवि
तबेलाको गन्ध सम्झेर आतुरिँदै
'बसन्त ! बसन्त !!' चिच्याइरहें
उजाड शिशिरमाथि उभिएर
फगत सुकेका पातहरू झर्दाको
बिरानो 'फड.....फड....' शब्द
रित्तो डालो हल्लाउँदै हरियो चरो उडेपछि
बिरानो एक्लो रूख
निर्जनतामा सुसाइरहेको ।

तल
बेँसीमा
कहराउँदै बगेको खोलालाई
मुठीभरिरमाछ्यालाई झैं
च्याप्प समातेर रअस्तित्व जाँच्दै
आफैभित्रको एक्लोपनका भुसहरू
निफन्न लागिपरें ।

धुजा-धुजा पार्दै
यो मैलो-अमिलो गन्हाउने सिरकर–हीनताबोधको
अनुभव गरिरहन्छु– बलिष्ठ विद्रोहको भुइँचालो
आफैमारबारम्बार
मांसल गीतका
नदी-कछ्याडहरूतिररलम्कँदै ।

पूर्णता !
तिम्रा अनतिक्रम्य मदमत्त टाकुराहरूलाई
कुल्चँदै
यिनै पयरले
एक दिनरअवश्य गुज्रनेछु – तिमीमाथिबाट ।

The poet inside whinnied, skittish,
imagining the smell of a stable
'Spring!' it neighed
stamping on winter's ground—
The dry syllable of leaves falling
against each other
As when a green bird lifts off a trembling branch
the soughing of the wind
in the tree of desolation

Grasping
by the fistful /
like a slithering fish / the loud river that flows
down the lowlands,
I examine existence
sifting the chaff of my own loneliness

Ripping this
rancid quilt to tatters / —wracked
with inadequacy—a great mutiny quakes
inside me / rumbling
down the floodplains of
a muscular song

Perfection!
Trampling these inviolable summits
of your intoxication
with these very soles
one day / I will pass—above you

कविताको कारखाना बन्द गरेर

कुइरोले डम्म छोपिराखेको
आफ्नै अवचेतनको गाउँतिर
ओर्लिरहेछु
सुस्त
सुस्त ।

Shutting the factory of poetry
I'm descending
slowly towards the fog-
shrouded village
of my subconscious

कायाकल्प : २

पातमा हात राखेँ मैले
पात पुतली बन्यो
र उडिरह्यो जन्म-जन्मान्तरसम्म ।

हावामा हात हल्लाएँ मैले
हावा परेवा बनेर भुर्र उड्नुपर्ने मेरो जादूलाई नटेरेर
पानी पो बन्यो ।
अनि कति जन्मअघि सुकेका लोककथाका पँधेराहरू
रसाउन थाले जताततै ।
अहिले पँधेर्नीहरूले पाखापखेरा घन्काउँदै
झिसमिसेको निद्रा बिथोलेर गाएका अजम्बरी गीतहरू
गुञ्जिरहेछन् मेरो अभ्यन्तरमा ।

उर्बर माटोमा मिसाएँ मैले
पितापुर्खाहरूले आर्जेको अनुभव केही,
केही सीप र अटल धैर्य ।
तर कुन्नि कस्तो विषाक्त विषादिको मायाजालमा
मुछिन पुगे –
माटो, अनुभव, सीप, अनि धैर्य ।
शुष्क बालुवामा पो अनुवाद हुँदै गए सबथोक
र मरूभूमीकरणको दूरागत शोकगीतमा
सुनिन थालेको छ शताब्दीको दुःखान्त अहिले ।

Metamorphosis—2

I placed my hand on a leaf
The leaf became a butterfly
and flew for ages.

I shook my fists in the wind
The air that should've transformed into a pigeon & flown
disregarded sorcery, turned to water instead.
And the wellsprings of folklore parched lifetimes ago
glistened everywhere.
Now the water bearers' undying songs resonant
on the hills unsettling twilight's slumber
echo inside me.

In the fertile earth I scattered
the forefathers' divine wisdom
their skill and infallible patience.
But who knows what toxic phantasmagoria
I've concocted—
soil, wisdom, skill, and patience.
They've all turned silently into sand
& in the desolate lament of the desert
the century's tragedy is beginning to be heard.

पितापुर्खाहरूले रचेर छाडेका
आफूभित्रको सङ्गीतलाई छोएँ सुस्तरी मैले ।
सङ्गीत आनन्दमा अनुभूतिकृत हुनुपर्नेमा
        सुस्केरामा पो डिकोड भयो,
अनि सुस्केराको कुटलिपिमा डिकोड भएको सङ्गीत
      फेरिँदै गयो सुस्त-सुस्त बाफमा ।

बाफ उड्दै-उड्दै गइरह्यो माथि, झन्माथि दिगन्ततिर
र बाफले चोला फेऱ्यो बादलको ।
बदल हेर्दा-हेर्दै रचिँदै गयो नीलिम आकाशमा
आकाश – अनेकौं अन्य आकाशहरूसँग हातेमालो गर्दै
                    गाभियो आकाशगङ्गामा ।
आकाशगङ्गा – अनगिन्ती आकाशगङ्गाहरूमा समाहित हुँदै
                    ब्यूँतियो ब्रह्माण्ड बनेर ।

ब्रह्माण्ड – खरबौं ब्रह्माण्डहरूको कोलाहलमा
            आफूलाई, आफू हुनुलाई खोज्दै
हुंइकिँदै गइरह्यो समयहीनताको सीमान्ततिर
जहाँ एउटा विकराल ब्ल्याकहोल ब्रह्माण्डलाई निल्न
            मुख बाइरहेको थियो अनादिमा ....

अनि म एक्कासि ऐँठनबाट
ब्यूँझन पुगेँ कहालिँदै
र आफ्नो अस्तित्वमा फिर्ता भएँ ॥

I touched the music inside me,
one that the forefathers wrote.
But instead of bringing me peace the music
unravelled into a sigh
Then the music that unravelled into the alphabet of sighs
further turned into mist.

The mist rose up, high above the horizon
and changed into clouds.
The clouds became more of themselves across the blue skies
The skies—clasped hands with other infinite skies
and became the milky way.
The milky way—merged with innumerable milky ways
and stirred as the cosmos.

The cosmos—amidst the cacophony of a billion other cosmoses
trying to become, trying to find itself
careened towards the edge of timelessness
where a grim blackhole opened its maw interminably
to swallow the cosmos whole...

When I came to suddenly
from a night-terror
and was returned to my own self again.

'म' तत्त्व अर्थात् छैठौं तत्त्व

माटो फर्कने छ माटोमै मक्ख पर्दै
पानी पानीतिरै जाने छ रमाउँदै
वायु वायुमै विलय हुनेछ नाच्दै-गाउँदै
अग्नि अग्निमै अलमलिने छ भरभराउँदै

अनि आकाशतत्त्व आकाशतिरै आकाशिने छ
भेट्न हतारिँदै नक्षत्रहरूलाई

तर 'म' – तत्त्व भने शास्त्रहरूले भन्ने गरे झैं
सक्किने छैन शून्यमा
रहिरहने छ रिक्तताहरूमा, सन्नाटाहरूमा,
सामसुम्महरूमा त्यो
प्रेम गर्नेहरूका स्मृतिमा, आँसुमा
अडिरहने छ सदाकाल

नयाँ पलाउने कलिला पालुवाहरूको हरियो उमङ्गमा
नयाँ फक्रने फूलका कोपिलाहरूका थरीथरी रङ्गमा
मौसमको पहिलो झरीको थोपा बनेर
ऋतुको पहिलो हिमपातको हिउँका फाल्सामा बौरिएर
पटक-पटक फर्किआउने छ 'म'–तत्त्व

समयको अनन्ततामा यसरी
सदासर्वदा रहिरहने छ
'म' – तत्त्व

The Sixth Element

Soil will return gladly to soil
Water will flow towards water joyously
Air will diffuse into air, singing and dancing
Fire will bewilder itself to raging fire

The Ether element will vapour skyward
impatient to join the constellations

But 'I'—the element, just as the scriptures say,
will never come to nothingness
In the lacunae, in the silences,
in the hush it will remain
In the reminiscences of lovers, in tears
it will endure

In the green hope of new leaves' sprout
In the bright unfurling of flower buds
As the first raindrop of the season
As awakening after the winter's frost
Time and again it will return—the 'I' element

In time's endlessness this way
always and forever it will exist
the 'I' element.

From *Anubhuti Yatrama*
(On a Journey through Intimations), 1990

अन्यमनस्कता

थामिए दिशाका दश रथहरू,
हुस्सुको चादर टक्टकाउँदी बिहानकी युवती ।

मेरो अन्यमनस्कताको तलाउमा
खित्काका ढुङ्गाहरू बर्साउँदै गइसके
चैतका चञ्चल ठिटीहरू ।

थाकेर ठिङ्ग उभिएका रूखका घोडाहरू
चारैतिर । भाषामा विदेशी शब्द झैं
घरमा अनायस भित्रिएका
अयाचित पाहुनाहरू ।

मभन्दा एक सय सात वर्ष बूढो
बोतल सैम्पेनको ।
एरिस्ट्रोक्रेटिक गफको चौरमा
पोलो खेल्ने साहब मित्रहरू ।
रण्डी झैं उदास दिउँसोको मुहार
कानमा साउती गर्न पल्केको अल्छी बतास ।

आज मलाई सञ्चो छ
बाहिरको अन्धकारमा अतीत
धूपीको रूख हराए हराए झैं ।
भो थुनिदिन्छु
यादतिर खुल्ने यो झ्याल पनि
निद्राको मोटो पर्दा तानी दिनु पऱ्यो सुती सुती ।

Inattention

The ten chariots of direction come to a halt,
morning's maiden shakes off the blanket of mist.

On the lake of my reverie
they've gone skipping pebbles of laughter,
the reckless girls of spring.

All around, the trees stand dead
still as beat horses. Like a foreign word in a language,
the house suddenly infiltrated
by unannounced visitors.

Hundred and seven years older than me,
a bottle of champagne.
On the field of aristocratic banter
my esteemed friends who play polo.
Sorrowful as an ageing whore the day's long face
& this idle breeze given to whisper rumours in its ears.

On this day I am relieved
the past lies outside in the darkening
pines, disappearing like pines in the dark.
Enough, let me close this
window opening towards another memory
pull as I sleep, sleep's thick curtain.

मोह

कुन्नि कुन मानसरोवरबाट थालियो
मेरो चेतनाको ब्रह्मपुत्र / र कुन्नि कति टाढा छ
समाप्तिको बङ्गोपसागर ?

दारिद्र्यसित डराएको माझी / र माझीसित
डराएका माछाहरू,
सपनासित झस्किएको नीद / र निद्रासित
कहालिएका आँखाहरू

ज्वारभाटाका दुवै हात जोरेर / नमस्कार,
चन्द्रमालाई, आकाशलाई-उद्वेलित समुद्रको ।

आकाशको दहभरि घोप्टाएर नीलो निःसीम मौनता,
ऊ कता लुक्यो कता ? / अभेद्य अन्तरिक्षको
मायावीयतातिर पो उसले / कतै ठोक्यो कि सुइँकुच्चा ?

झरीमा लुछुप्प रूझेको भदौको इन्द्रकमल रात,
त्यसै रातसित जोरिएका अनेक स्मृतिखण्ड / किम्वदन्ती,
देह-सुवास ।

मनको निर्जन वनमा / ओल्लो छेउदेखि पल्लो छेउसम्म
कुन्नि को गयो हिंडेर अज्ञात ।

Spell

Who knows where the Brahmaputra of my consciousness
began, from what Mansarovar on high / & how far
the bay of its emptying?

The boatman fears poverty / & the fish
fear the boatman
Sleep startled by dreams / & eyes
stricken with sleep

The tides join their palms together / Salutations!
to the moon, to the sky—from the churning sea

Spilling a boundless blue silence over the sky's great flare,
where has he hidden, where? / through fabric impenetrable
did he hotfoot it / into the illusion of the atmosphere?

Night of gardenia blooms drenched in September rain
Yoked to this night other memory rooms / mythical
body-fragrant

In the heart's bereft forest / from one end to the other end
Who walked by unnamed

सूर्य शिकार

यहींनेर आएर सिद्धिन्छ अग्नि-युगको
कथा । चेतनाका मायावी सुरूङ्हरूमा
सूर्य शिकार भएका हाम्रा पुर्खाहरूको
पाइलाको ध्वनि / या कुनै खण्डहरहरू
जसको भर पर्न मान्छे डराउँछ / त्यहीं
एउटा नदी उमारेर बाँच्नलाई
अत्तालिन्छ मन ।

ओ मेरी आमा !
म जहाँ छु त्यहाँ नक्षत्रका नाम
छैनन् । न त्यहाँ कुनै क्षितिज फेला पर्छ
आकाशबाहेक / म त्यहाँ
आदिम पलायनलाई बोकेर घस्रिरहेको छु
आफूभित्रभित्रै । अँध्यारो उज्यालो त्यहाँ
एकअर्कामा खप्टिन घस्रिरहेका छन्
अजर समयको विस्तारमा ।

ओल्लो छेउदेखि पल्लो छेउसम्म अन्तरिक्षको
त्यहाँ कुनै अर्थ लाग्दैन / ओ आमा ! म जहाँ छु ।

ओ आमा !
त्यहाँ कुनै यथार्थ बूढो हुँदैन / फेरिनु –
बाहेक । त्यहाँ भित्रिन निषेध छ दुःखलाई ।
तन्नेरी सुख त्यहाँ जस्ताको तस्तै रहिरहन्छ / कहिल्यै
छिप्पिँदैन ।

Sunhunt

Here is where the tale of the fiery age
ends. Sunhunted in the illusory tunnels of consciousness
the echoes of our ancestors' footsteps
linger / or some derelict ruins
deserted by humans / there the heart quickens
to divine a surging river
and live.

Oh mother!
Where I live now there are no names
for the constellations. No horizon in sight
except the ancient sky / a primitive escape
weighed on my back, I am dragging
myself inward. Light and darkness
graze against each other
in time's expanse.

From one end of the universe to the other
no meaning cumulates / oh mother! where I live now.

The present doesn't age / only changes hands—
with another present. Suffering isn't welcome.
Tender happiness stays unchanged / unspoiled.

खोजेर डायनोसरको फोसिलमा
आफ्ना पुर्खाहरूको गन्ध / हतासिएका
हाम्रा हातहरूको कथा / अब म
बयान गर्दै जानेछु। हामीमास्तिर
आकाश नरहला / अन्तरिक्षको अड्कल नरहला,
उज्यालो अँध्यारोको निःशब्द विस्तार नरहला,
तर यत्ति भन्नु छ –
"मान्छेको कथा पृथिवीमा फेरि पनि / रहनुपर्छ
बाँचेको।"

Tracing the scent of my ancestors
among the jurassic fossils / I will now
recount / the tale of our defeated
hands. The skies won't loom
above us forever / neither the approximation of the universe,
nor the endless play of light and dark,
but I'll say this,
'On this earth must continue to live / the tale
of the human tribe.'

इच्छा-पत्र

घरबाट भागेकी अल्लारे ठिटी जस्तै
हतारिएको ऋतु
अनि उद्विग्न उदास म ।

आफैबाट गुमेका दिनहरू
गीत भएछन् चालै नपाई / अरू कसैका कण्ठका ।
आफैबाट उम्केका शब्दहरू
बैरीको हातमा –
मैलाई ठुन्काउने हतियार ।

यसबेला ममाथि जुन समय
टाँगिएको छ –
त्यो तिम्रो मुस्कान जस्तो छैन
मलाई घोप्न ताकेको छुरा जस्तो छ ।

त्यै पनि म नम्रताको स्वाङ गर्दिनँ
भद्र औपचारिकता देखाउँदिनँ पटक्कै ।
मर्न परे पनि म खुशी छु 'उफ' नभनी
आफ्नै कट्टरता मलाई प्रिय छ ।

अब,
केवल यत्ति चाहन्छु :
"प्रकृति र ऋतुहरूले मलाई नछलून्, नछक्काऊन्;
म मर्दाको दिन
घाम लागेको होस् / फूलहरू फक्रेकै देखिऊन् ।"

Wish-Letter

Like a runaway girl fleeing home
the season jittery with haste
& me baffled sad

Unbeknown to me, days that I had lost
turned into songs / in someone else's throat
Words that escaped me
fell in the hands of the Enemy—
now a weapon to splinter me

This moment in time that is tethered
above me now—
it is quite unlike your smile
Like a dagger it is aimed to plunge into me

Even so, I will feign neither politeness
nor tact or formality
I will die without an 'ah' if I have to
My mulish pride dear to me

Here,
I only wish this:
'Let nature and the seasons neither cheat nor deceive me,
On the day that I die
May the sun be out / the flowers' unfurling be seen.'

अर्कै मान्छे

चिल टोपी झैं आएर
बस्छ / घरको टाउकोमा ।
सैम्पेनको बोतल झैं/ब्लास्ट हुन्छ
मनको आवेग । अनि फ़िंज झैं
छोडिजान्छ कविता / सुक्नलाई
घाममा ।

विचारको पुरानो कमेज
समयको बतासले उडाउँछ ।
रूमाल बनी थन्कूँ थन्कूँ झैं लाग्ने
इच्छाहरू / कसैको हातको मुठीमा
कस्सिएर / अब मित्रसेनका गीत झैं
थोत्रा पुराना लाग्न थाले ।

म आफैंमा / कुनै अर्कै मान्छे झैं
खप्टिएर / रिङिरहन्छु
शहरभरि सडकभरि ।

The Other Man

A hawk swoops in like a hat
perches / on the house's skull.
Like a champagne bottle / blasts
open, the heart's impulsions. Like froth
it leaves a poem / out to dry
in the sun.

The old shirt of my ideologies
blows in the barbed wind of time.
Desires / like a handkerchief
smothered / in someone's clenched fist
fossilized like the dreary songs
of Mitrasen.

Stacked above myself / like another
man / in a fugue I wander
        the city, the streets.

यदि म...

यदि म एउटा पुल भएको भए / अन्धकारको
नदीमा टाँगी माग्थें आफैंलाई / र उज्यालोलाई
उज्यालोसित जोरिदिन्थें
यसरी ।

If I Were

If I were a bridge I would ask
to be fastened across the river of darkness
then I could join the passage
from light   to light

अनुपस्थिति तिम्रो

लिपिएको आँगनमा
कुन्नि कसका पाइलाका डोब ?
तिमी छैनौ गौंथली झैं
उड्छन् मनमा हज्जार अपसोच ।

Your Absence

In the dung-paved yard
impression of whose footprints?
You aren't here   Like the swallows
a thousand misgivings lift off in my heart

मेरा कविताहरू

मुलुक मार्न हैन / तिम्रो हिसी परेको मुहारको
सम्मोहनबाट मुक्त हुन
कविता लेख्थें ।

अचेल, आफूभित्र जुन आगो छ / शोषण, दमन
र सङ्घर्षलाई बुझ्नेदेखि दन्कन थालेको आगो,
त्यसैको रापलाई व्यक्त गर्न
कविता लेख्छु ।

My Poems

Not to reign over a nation / but to be liberated
from the spell of your immaculate face
I used to write poems.

These days, there is a fire inside me / fire that rages
in the knowledge of suffering and oppression,
to manifest the shimmering heat of that fire
I write poems.

पीडाको रूख

तिम्रा आँखाको भुमरीमा रिङिरहें फन्फनी / युगौं ।
म पीडाको रित्तो बोट बनें / मोहको फूल
नदीमा खसेदेखि ।

Tree of Pain

In the whirlpool of your eyes I spiralled / for ages.
I became a skeletal tree of pain / after the flower
of desire's fugue fell in the river below.

कुन्नि कुन अपरिचित गाउँकी नयनतारा बरूवा

(फरवरी १९८३ मा असममा निरापराध मारिनेहरूको नाममा)

रिहा-मेखेलामा सजिएकी
कुन्नि कुन गाउँकी नयनतारा बरूवा
सधैं आउँछिन् मेरा सपनामा
र भन्ने गर्छिन्–
आऊ न, एउटा नयाँ जिन्दगी उमारौं
यहाँका खेतहरूमा
उत्साहका नयाँ गीत सुसेलौं हामी दुबै मिली
यहाँका परिचित रनवनमा ।

कुन्नि कुन गाउँकी नयनतारा बरूवा
साउँताली लोकगीतका धूनहरूमा ब्यूझिन्छिन् मभित्र
र मलाई डोऱ्याएर लैजान्छिन्
वसन्तहरूतिर, फूलहरूतिर
अनि मध्यरातमा मुटु चिरिने गरी रूने
केतेकी चराका उदास गीतहरूतिर ।

तिमीलाई कसरी सम्झाऊँ नयनतारा !
मसित फुर्सद छैन – वसन्तका फूलहरूसित छिल्लिने
वसन्तको बताससँग गफ्फिने
अहिले यहाँ हुरी चल्दैछ – म बाहिर / मभित्र ।
सल्किरहेछन् शहरहरू, जलिरहेछन् गाउँहरू
गिद्धहरूले ढाकिएको छ हामीमाथिको आकाश, नयनतारा !

कुन्नि कुन अपरिचित गाउँकी नयनतारा बरूवा,
डफला लोकनर्तकीहरूको समूह नृत्यबाट मलाई चियाउँछिन्

Of Some Unidentified Village, Nayantara Barua

(In memory of the lives lost in the Nellie Massacre in Assam, February 1983)

Adorned in Riha-mekhela,
Nayantara Barua, of some unidentified village,
comes to me in a dream each night
and says—
Come, grow a new life with me
here in these fields murmuring
a new song of ardour
in this land we know.

Of some unidentified village, Nayantara Barua
stirs awake inside me to the rhythm of a Santhali tune
and leads me by the hand
towards spring, towards the flowers
and at midnight towards the heart-rending cry
of the brainfever's inconsolable birdsong.

How do I explain to you, Nayantara!
I don't have the leisure—to fiddle with the flowers of spring,
to join the laughter riding the new wind.
There is a storm brewing here—inside me and outside.
The cities are being torched, the villages blazing
the vultures darken the sky above us, Nayantara!

Of some unidentified village, Nayantara Barua
steals a look through the weave of Dafla dancers

र आमन्त्रणका असङ्ख्य कटाक्षहरूले मोहनी लाउँछिन् ।
उनलाई के थाहा
मान्छेलाई मनपर्छ मान्छेको आखेट
मान्छेलाई मनपर्छ मान्छेको मासु ।

बज्दैछ मादल, बज्दैछ ढोल
नाच्दैछन् खुट्टा, हाँस्दैछन् आँखा
जलिरहेछन् गाउँ, बजिरहेछन् बुट
कवाज खेल्दै हिंडिरहेछन् शिकारीहरू ।

उजाडिँदैछन् घर, चिहिरिँदैछन् खेतबारी
रूँदैछन् नदी, भत्किँदैछन् पुलहरू
बज्दैछन् मादल, नाच्दैछन् खुट्टा
आलापविलापले भरिएका ट्रकहरूले
काटिरहेछन् मध्यरातमा सुटुक्क सिमाना ।

मध्यरातमा आखेट गर्न निस्कन्छन् ट्रकहरू
अनि हराउँछन् हर्कध्वज गाउँबूढाका जाहान
अनि भेटिन्छ बलात्कारले मरेकी मालतीको लाश
डिङ्गाहरूसित सल्काइन्छन् गोठहरू
आँखाहरूसितै जलाइन्छन् सपनाहरू
सशरीर डढाइन्छन् इच्छाहरू

राँको बालेर हिँडिरहेको जुलूसमाझबाट
शङ्खध्वनि झैं निस्केर मभित्र गाडिंदै जान्छिन्
कुन्नि कुन अपरिचित गाउँकी नयनतारा बरूवा

'गहपुर' हो कि 'नेली' हो
'राजबारी' हो कि 'जहामारी'

lures me with her countless stolen glances.
Oh, what does she know
of men who like to hunt men
of men who hunger for the flesh of men.

The drums beat, the cymbals clang
the feet begin to dance, the eyes begin to laugh
the villages keep burning, the boots keep thudding
the hunters march, setting their devious traps.

Homes uprooted, the fields are torn
the rivers weep, the bridges collapse
the drums beat, the feet begin to dance
the trucks full of lamentation
steal through the border at midnight.

At midnight, the trucks patrol the villages
and the village chief's wife vanishes without a trace
and they find Malati's raped body left for dead.
The blowflies torched with the cowsheds
Dreams scorched with the eyes
Desires burnt with the bodies.

Amidst the throng of torch-bearing picketers
like the shrill note of a blown conch shell she pierces me
Nayantara Barua of some unidentified village.

Is it Gohpur or Nellie,
Rajbari or Jahamari?

दिउँसै हिँड्छन् कालो घोडामा चढेर वनझाँक्री
एकाबिहानै निस्कन्छन् घरहरूबाट हिँस्रक नरभक्षीहरू
मुखमा रगतको स्वाद, हातमा खुँडा , आँखामा विक्षिप्त घृणा
मान्छेका रगतको मात चढेका मान्छेहरू ।

कस्तो बोक्सीले टोके झैं नीलडाम बोकेका सपनाहरू
अपुताली परेको घरमा ओत लाग्न आएका
यी हुचिल कराएजस्ता वीभत्स दुःस्वप्नहरू ।

मुगा मेखेला चादरमा सजिएर सलज्ज मलाई हेरिरहेकी
कुन्नि कुन अपरिचित गाउँकी नयनतारा बरूवा
मलाई आफ्ना निष्कपट मुस्कानका नामघरहरूतिर डोऱ्याउँछिन्
मलाई आफ्ना निष्पाप आमन्त्रणका नदी घाटहरूमा बोलाउँछिन् ।

तिमीलाई कसरी सम्झाऊँ नयनतारा !
हृदयभन्दा ठूलो सत्य मेरो निम्ति अरू केही छैन ।
तर हृदयविदारक यथार्थका घाइते दृश्यहरू
तिमी र ममाझ विशाल नदी बनी प्रवाहित छ यसबेला
म फड्केर पारि जान सक्दिनँ
तिमी पौडेर वारि आउन सक्दिनौ ।

नयनतारा ! तिमीलाई कसरी सम्झाऊँ :
"हृदयभन्दा ठूलो सत्य मेरो निम्ति अरू केही छैन ।"

In broad daylight the shaman rides a black horse
at the break of dawn the cannibals steal out of their hovels
taste of blood in mouth, machetes in hand, eyes lit with rage
men drunk on the blood of men.

What dreams are these blue-bruised by a witch's gnaw,
what curse come to roost in a barren house
these nightmares like the screech of falcons.

Draped in a chador of Mekhela silk, glancing coyly,
Nayantara Barua, of some unidentified village,
leads me to the prayer hall of her guileless smile
beckons me to the riverbank of her sinless invitation.

How do I make you understand, Nayantara!
There is no bigger truth for me than that of the heart.
But the mutilated scenes from this harrowing time
flow like a massive channel between us.
I cannot wade to the other side
you cannot swim through to this side.

Nayantara! How do I make you understand:
There is no bigger truth than that of the heart.

ब्लूज

रात्रिको भायोलिनमा / ब्लूजको सुर
मनौं हिक्का काढ्दै रोइरहेछ अन्धकार / कृष्णवर्णी
निग्रो विह्वलता । छातीमा भत्कन्छ कविताको
लय / उनीहरूलाई सम्झँदा । चस्कन्छ कुन्नि
कहाँनिर मान्छे / मान्छेको विरूद्ध ।

कोर्राको प्रहारले उप्किएको / पिठ्युँको मासु,
डामैडाम छापिएको छाला । सारा रात पीडासित लुकामारी खेल्छ
निद्रा । कालो शरीर भएका मान्छेहरू / चिच्याइरहन्छन् दुखाइ
बिर्सन । सल्बलाइरहन्छन् झुप्राहरूमा गडयौंला झैं ।
उनीहरूका आँखामा झुण्डिएको छ लालटिन जस्तै / ध्वाँसो पोतिएको
बिरामी जून / अनि धुजाधुजा भइसकेको एउटा जर्जर
आकाश ।

कालो वेदना / अनि कालो नै उज्यालो । अनि निक्खुर
कालो चेतना / हब्सी सूर्य,
अनि हब्सी रङ्गका नक्षत्रहरू ।
कमाराकमारीहरू / आफ्नै दुःखको अँध्यारोमा छेलिएर
रातको मृत शिशुलाई काखमा राखी
चिहिरिँदै गाइरहेछन् ब्लूज ।

The Blues

Often it is in English which is like a howl, or a shout, or a machine-gun, or the wind, or a wave. It is also like the blues.

—Kamau Brathwaite, 'The History of the Voice'

On the night's violin / the drone of blues is the sobbing
darkness itself / a bluegod-hued delirium.
In my chest breaks the metre
of a song / when I think of them. Somewhere
a man being goaded by another man.

Flesh peeling off whipped backs,
skin trenched with welts. All night sleep plays hide
and seek with agony. Dark-skinned men shouting
to forget pain. In their shacks they squirm like earthworms.
In their eyes, like a lantern, hangs a sick soot-
streaked moon / against an ancient tattered
sky.

Black anguish / and the black bright. Pitch
black consciousness / a black sun,
and a black constellation.
Sheltered under the darkness of their own despair
cradling the night's dead child
piercingly, the slaves sing the blues.

वातावरणमा रन्किन्छ आर्तनाद । छ्याप्पिन्छ
विषाद-बाग्मतिदेखि धनशिरीसम्म / सेनेगलदेखि
युफ्रिटिसम्म / ड्रमदेखि मृदङ्गसम्म ।

क्रमशःलम्कँदै आइरहेछ
उज्यालो...

A cry of distress heats the air. Sorrow looms—
from the river Bagmati to Dhansiri / from Senegal
to Euphrates / from the drums to the mridanga.

Then—slow, slouching
comes light...

ओ मेरा सूर्य पीडाहरू !

प्रवचन झैं पवित्र / उनको मुहारलाई
सम्झेर, मैले अन्तरिक्ष ताकेर उडाइदिएँ
आफूमा गुँड लगाई बसेका / जम्मै आवेगका परेवाहरू

कहिले कतै म आफैलाई अतिक्रमण गर्छु / अनि
कहिले कतै आफैंमा उभिएर
आफैंलाई फड्कन्छु / तर समुद्रबाट बुद्रुक्क उफ्रेको माछो
फेरि समुद्रमा खसे झैं म खस्छु / आफैमा ।

धेरै पटक म तिमी हुन चाहन्छु / तर रहन्छु
म नै / मादक भ्रममा अल्मलिंदै म / आफैलाई
उद्‌भिद् देख्ने प्रयास गर्छु / एउटा कमिलोमा
ओछ्याउन खोज्छु आफ्नो सत्ता ।

ए मेरा सूर्य पीडाहरू !
मलाई थाहा छ मेरो अस्तित्व
प्रोटोप्लाज्मको दुर्भेद्य रहस्य हो ।

कहिले कतै म आफैलाई एउटा
पुरानो र जर्जर अन्तरिक्ष महसूस गर्छु / मैले
खप्न नसकेका पीडाहरू जम्मै
पौराणिक नक्षत्र झैं / ब्लेक होलमा
फेरिंदै जाँदै छन् त्यहाँ ।

Oh My Sun Griefs!

Remembering her face / sacred
as a sermon, I aimed for the stars
& released the pigeons of yearning / brooding inside me.

Sometimes I trespass against myself / and
sometimes I stand over myself
and stomp on it / but like a fish escaped out of sea
falls back into sea I fall back / into myself.

Sometimes I wish to be you / but I remain
only myself / bewildered in an intoxicated delusion / I see
myself as verdure / upon an ant
I want to spread my being.

Oh my sun griefs!
I know my existence
is the protoplasm's inexplicable riddle.

Sometimes I consider myself
an ancient, decrepit cosmos / and there
my unbearable griefs all
like a mythical constellation / collapse
into black holes.

कविता

भाषाको राजधानीमा
अक्षरका नागरिकहरू
शब्दको भवनमा
सुरक्षित छैनन् अब ।

कहिले वाक्यको विद्रोह
कहिले लिपिको जगजगी ।
कहिले फेरि अर्थको चेतावनी
अर्थहीनताको नारा र
प्रतीक तथा विम्बको
आफ्नो हकको मागमा
गुप्त षड्यन्त्रका योजनाहरू

म यिनमा कतै सामेल छैन ।
[खै कसरी भनूँ?
खै कुन मुखले...?]

Poem

In the kingdom of language
The citizens of alphabet
Are no longer safe
In the palace of words.

Sometimes the revolt of a sentence
Sometimes the script's riot.
Sometimes meaning's warning cry
Against the loud protest of meaninglessness
Symbol and Image both
Grapple for their rights
Scheming a secret conspiracy.

I'm not at all a part of this.
[How do I say this?
... with what face?]

From *Samvedna, O Samvedna!* (Intimations, Oh Intimations!), 1981

उही शहर : उही नदी

उही शहरको थकित अनुहार / अँध्यारोका
पैंतलाले कुल्चिएर गएका गल्लीहरू ।
विस्थापितको फुस्रो अनुहार झैं देखिने / लाइटपोस्टका
केही पुराना बल्ब । जिन्दगी,
फ्यूज हुने क्षणको कुराइमा ।

बतास झैं टाँगिएर कुनै अग्लो तालको
रूखमा झसङ्गिनु । आफूबाटै हिंडिसकेका
आग्रहहरूलाई छाम्दा पनि संवेदना नभेट्नु ।
आफूलाई आफ्नै हत्केलाले छुन खोज्नु ।
छोप्नु । घोप्टिनु शिरीषको छाया झैं
आफैमुनि ।

यी सबै सुस्त-सुस्त हुँदै जान्छ । आफूबाट
आफू अनुपस्थित रहँदा । बिर्संदा आफैलाई
यी सबैथोक बेहोर्न सहज हुन्छ ।

अनि यस्तैमा एकदिन हठात् लाग्ने छ
यही शहरको छेउबाट एउटा नदी पनि बग्ने गर्छ ।

Same City, Same River

The city's tired face / alleys
trampled on by the heels of darkness.
Like an exile's grimy face / the lamp post's
old bulb. Life itself
waiting to be blown out.

To be startled like the wind
caught in the high trees. To be oblivious to touch
the prayers that have long walked out of me.
To want to caress yourself with your own palm.
To cover yourself. To spill like the shade of the mimosa tree
underneath yourself.

Gradually these things begin to transpire. When
you are absent from yourself. Easy to accept this
when you forget yourself.

Then one day you notice, all at once
beside this city, a river also flows.

नगरी

अझ एउटा अपवित्र अँध्यारोमा डुबेको
रात। सम्भोग-मुद्राका छायाँहरू सम्झनामा।
बिर्साइको बाटो कुर्दा-कुर्दै कुजिएका
इच्छाहरू।

साउतीकी अभ्यस्त कुनै ठिटी झैं
साँझ / सुटुक्क आएर अल्पिएपछि
सम्पूर्ण नगरी ममा आई ब्यूँझन्छ।
मात लागेर चेत नपाएका रक्स्याहाहरूको
धङ्धङाउँदो शरीर झैं / छायाँको भुँडी बोकेका
टोलभरिका अमेल-अमेल घरहरू / आँखाबाट
चेतनासम्म स्थापित।

सफल अप्रेसनपछिको डाक्टर झैं / आश्वस्त
कहिल्यै हुन नसकिने जिन्दगीबाट।
विधवालाई चुराको रहर झैं मेरा कामनाहरू
सधैं लथालिङ्ग / चाँदीको हस्कोबिना।
हो, मलाई सपना स्थगित गर्ने बानी
लागेको छ / आफैले स्थगित गर्दै आएका
यी स्याहारहीन सपनाहरूरशह / बाट
चिहानमाथि बिनावसन्त फुलेको / सानो
फूलको मुस्कानसम्म स्थापित।

City

Drowning in a second, desecrated darkness—
the night. In the mind, shadows form gestures of coitus.
Wants crushed under the interminable wait
for oblivion.

Dusk falls like a young girl adept at whispering
secrets / after its silent vanishing
the whole city walks into me & awakes.
Like the tremoring body of an alcoholic
in withdrawal / carrying a belly of shadows
the town's mismatched houses / erected from the eyes
to the consciousness.

Like a surgeon victorious after sewing someone back up /
never reassured by life again.
Like a widow's longing for bangles, my desires
in disarray / without the reek of silver.
Yes, I've taken to the habit of deferring
dreams / I've deferred myself
in these derelict dreams / erected
from the city to the tiny flower / unfurling
on a grave in the absence of spring.

मृत्यु

शरीरको नदीमा जब
कथित आत्माको माछा थाक्छ
जिन्दगीलाई बिसाउन मन लाग्छ
मृत्युको चौतारामा । कतै
केही हुँदैन / नदी छट्पटाउँछ
माछा अन्यमनस्क बन्छ / बस् ।

वातावरणले कातरता ओढेको बेला
मौन समूहमा कतिपय अस्फूट शब्दहरू
पौडन्छन् / प्रार्थनाका करूण शब्दहरू ।

शेषमा रहन्छ केवल प्रार्थना,
मौन प्रार्थना !

Death

In the body's river when
the fish of the soul is tired
life wants to rest
in the pitstop of death. Nothing
transpires / only the river is restless
the fish distracted

When the air wears a shroud of cowardice
in a silent horde / indistinct words
swim to surface / mournful words of invocation

What's left—
a mute prayer.

कन्ट्रास्ट

I love you and you know it—this at least,
This comfort is mine own in all my pain.
—Christina Rossetti

मरूभूमिको छातीमा घाम झैं /
पोखिने भए तिम्रो मुस्कान / अनायास मेरो
वरिपरि / शायद मेरो सामर्थ्य डुँडो हुने थिएन ।

वातावरणभरि उम्रन सक्छन् / अनिच्छाका
सिउँडीहरू / जब जाडोका रातहरू झैं लम्मिन थाल्छन्
रूख्याईंका क्षणहरू । कुनै शब्द, कुनै मन्त्र
अचूक हुने छैनन् त्यसबेला / घृणा
अमोघ बन्दै जानेछ ।

म छट्पटाउँछु–निद्रामा 'सपना' झैं / म
गुम्सिन्छु –क्लोरोफर्मको गन्धमा 'होस' झैं / कुनै
नदीको बालुवालाई मुठ्याएर चिच्च्याउन मन लाग्दैछ –
म पनि ढुंगा थिएँ कुनै दिन इतिहासका / मेरो आजको
यथार्थ यही बालुवा हो / जहाँ मेरो
परिश्रमको घाम सुस्ताउने गर्छ /
आफ्नै छायामुनि थिच्चिएर ।

Incongruity

What are heavy? Sea-sand and sorrow.
—Christina Rossetti

If only like the sun scorching the desert's breast
your smile would / suddenly pour
all around me / maybe my strength wouldn't ebb

The cactus of reluctance in the air
grows / when like a winter's night
the barren moment elongates   No word
no incantation can fix this / only contempt
grows

Restless—like a dream inside sleep / I am
stifled—like consciousness inside a breath of chloroform / I want
to grasp a fistful of sand from the riverbank and scream—
I too was a stone of history once / today
my reality is this sand / where
burdened by my own shadow / the long
sun of my toil sets

नदी-राग – १

कावेरी : तिमीभित्र प्राचीन सुरूंग जस्तै रहस्यमय
विस्तार जो तिमीलाई महसूस
भइरहन्छ / जान्दछ्यौ त्यो मेरो
संवेदनाको ब्याकूल छाया हो ।

River Raga—1

Kaveri! Like an ancient subterranean tunnel
the mysterious expanse inside you
that you sense / Can you tell
it is but the tormented shadow of my intimation.

नदी-राग – २

ब्याकूल मेरा रहरका छायाहरूको
नदी एउटा बग्छ । नदीमा
माछाहरू रंग-विरंगी उत्कण्ठाहरूका ।
यसरीनै बगेर हुत्तिंदै गए / जन्म-जन्मान्तरका
कथाहरू / कहिल्यै नदेखिएको
रहस्यको सागरतिर ।

तिर्खाएका छन् अझै पनि
पानीका थोपाहरू – यी मेरा
आजन्म कामनाका । डढेर घाममा
अतृप्तिको ।

भो अब प्रेम नखोज्
ओ मेरो आहत मन !
ढुंगामा लेउ पलाउँछ
फूल त्यहाँ फक्रँदैन ।

River Raga—2

Tormented, a river flows made of the shadows
of my longing. In the river
are the variegated fish of my agonies.
This is how the infinite lore of the ages flows
in the current / towards the indiscernible
ocean of mystery.

Parched still
the waters—of my lifelong
desires. Cindered in the sun
of my discontent.

Enough, don't search for love
battered heart!
Algae grows on rocks
flowers don't bloom there.

अन्तरीप – १

हब्शी-रात
लोलाउँछ आँखा-आँखामा ।
सल्कन्छन् आँखामा
अविश्वासका चुरोटहरू ।

जहाँ एकान्तले बिर्सिन्छ आफ्नो
नाम / नदीले आफ्नो रूप
त्यही अन्तरीप हो ।

ओ इरावती !
कुन अन्कन्टारमा बगाएर लुकाई राखेकीछ्यौ
घृणा / कहाँ छ तिम्रो अमांसल प्रेमको
अजान अन्तरीप ?

एउटा नीलनक्षत्र अझै पनि चम्कने गर्छ
अक्कासको विह्वल छातीमा / पीडाको
मन्त्रमा डुबेका रातहरूमा ।

Headland—1

Black core of night
dousing the eyes with sleep.
Each hollow eye lit
with cigarettes of disbelief.

The place where solitude forgets
its own name / the river its form
there is a headland.

Oh Irawati!
Into what interiors have you swept away and hidden
contempt / where is your emaciated love's
unknown headland?

A blue constellation still glimmers
across the sky's breast of disquiet / in the nights
drowned in pain's sacred speech.

अन्तरीप – २

कुनै दन्त्यकथाको देशमा भित्रिने
अँध्यारो सुरूंगलाई छाम्दै / झुक्किएर
तिमी त्यस अन्तरीपमा पुग्न सक्ने छौ ।
त्यहाँ डम्म घाम लागेको हुनेछ
समयको आंगमा ।

टहटह जून लागेको अँध्यारा रातहरूमा / सुखले
विचलित भएको मान्छे झैं आवेगिन्छन् / नरिवलका
दैत्य रूखहरू / बतासको छातीमा ।
समयको फुलमा ओथ्रा बसेकी / जिज्ञासाको पोथी
कुखुरा झोंक्रिरहन्छे / अनागत सम्झेर ।

जहाँ समुद्रले बिर्सन्छ / आफ्नो स्थिति,
जहाँ माटोले बिर्सन्छ / आफ्नो नाम, त्यही
अन्तरीप हो । अझै पनि हक्कानिन्छ / त्यहाँको
नीरवता कसैले चर्को बोल्दा धरी ।
अनेक डुंगाले जहाँ निस्तब्धता
ओसारिरहन्छन् दिउँसोपख / त्यहीं
निदाउन देऊ तिम्रो जागरणलाई ।

निद्राको समुद्रमा सपनाको सानो डुंगा
बिर्साइको देश खोज्दै डुलिरहन्छ । कुन्नि कुन
कटिबन्धमा पर्छ त्यो अन्तरीप / जहाँ
घामको न्यानो स्पर्श / सधैं-सधैंलाई
आफ्नो हुनेछ – मुटुमा तिम्रो नाम झैं ।

Headland—2

Feeling your way through a dark tunnel
into some mythical kingdom / you may arrive
at the headland unaware.
There will be blazing sun
                    on the bare back of time.

On bright moonlit nights / unnerved like a man
distracted by happiness / the demonic palm
trees / thrash in the wind's breast.
The hen of curiosity / sits on time's egg
brooding / what will not arrive.

Where the sea forgets / its own condition,
where the soil forgets / its name, there is
a headland. Where silence scatters
even as someone raises their voice to speak.
In the afternoon, where the stones ferry
stillness / let your vigil
rest there.

In the sea of sleep a pebble of dream
drifts in search of a forgotten realm. Who knows
what latitude it falls in, this headland / where
the sun's warm touch / is yours
interminably—as your name inside me.

From *Parewa: Seto Kala*
(Pigeons: White, Black), 1977/1984

व्यर्थता

धूलोले बतासमा
आफ्नो अनुहार बनाउन खोज्छ / मैले
तिमीमा ।

न धूलो नै सफल भयो आजसम्म
न म ।

Futility

The dust wants to draw its face
on the wind / I
on you

Neither the dust gets it right
nor will I

स्वगत

अर्थभन्दा पर बाँच्ने मोह
राख्दिनँ म । शब्दोत्तर पनि
अस्तित्व छ कि अर्थको
खोज्दैछु । मलाई खोज्न देऊ ।

मलाई खन्न देऊ सुस्केरा / उच्छ्वास ।
पीडाका अनन्य भूमिगत आवास ।
मलाई खोज्नदेऊ निःशब्द । शब्दहीन
अनुभूति ।

Aside

I do not desire to live
far from meaning   whether meaning stirs
outside of words—I'm trying
to find   let me seek

Let me dig, exhale
                    breathbloom
the many subterranean rooms of anguish
allow me to search without speech
some wordless intimation

कलाकार / सागर / सिम्फोनी

सिम्फोनीहरू सागरका उत्ताल लहरमा ।
जहाँ नींदमा सपनाका जहाज यात्रामा निस्कन्छन् ।
चेतनाको मस्तूलमा समुद्रको चीसो बतास ।

सिम्फोनी केवल सिम्फोनी । सिम्फोनी : जहाँ बिथोवन
पीडाले रोइरहन्छन् / मोजार्ट पनि त हाँस्न
सक्दैनन् बिचरा । कलाकार कति असहाय हुन्छ ।
सिम्फोनी दिन्छ, सट्टामा केवल आँसु लिन्छ ।
माया हैन । [कसले हालिदिने अपनत्वको एक मुठी
भिक्षा / कलाकारको मुटुको भिक्षा पात्रमा ।]

सिम्फोनीहरू सागरको उत्ताल लहरमा
सिम्फोनी केवल सिम्फोनी ।

Artist / Ocean / Symphony

Symphonies hidden in the sea's giant waves
where the tall ships of dreams launch into.
Cold sea winds fill the sails of consciousness.

Symphony's only a symphony: where
Beethoven weeps in agony / poor Mozart
is inconsolable too. How terribly feeble artists are.
Symphonies in exchange for tears.
Never love. (Who will drop a handful of intimacy
in the artist's bowl of alms)

Symphonies hidden in the sea's giant waves.
Symphony only symphony.

मेरो स्वर्ग

दस्तूरमै बाँधिएको छु
म पनि तिमी जस्तै ।
साङ्ला यी विवशता हैनन्
मेरा निम्ति ।
एक्यूरिएम त माछाको विश्व हो ।
सागर : स्वर्गको कल्पना ।

मेरो एक्यूरिएम– यो समाज,
समाजका दस्तूर ।
तिमी, तिम्रो माया :
मेरो स्वर्गको कल्पना ।

Of Heaven

Bound by customs
I'm just like you.
But these fetters you see
aren't helplessness.
An aquarium is a whole universe for the fish.
Ocean, its imagined heaven.

My aquarium—this world
and its customs.
You, your love:
my invention of heaven.

प्रमिथियसको सुस्केरा

कठै, उज्यालो ओसार्दा-ओसार्दै
काठ भइसके यी मेरा दुई हात ।
तर कहिल्यै ननिखिने सृष्टिभरिको
यो बाक्लो अँध्यारो रात ।

यसै छायाँसम्भव रात्रिको कुनै कीलामा
झुन्याएर शिथिलता
झकाउनसम्म पाएहुन्थ्यो म पनि एक्कैछिन । अझ
कति टोलाइरहूँ म यसरी
निद्राको डिल-डिलमा पुस्ता-पुस्ता ।

अब त सृष्टिभरिका आँखा उघारिनुपर्छ
एक-एक गरी । विश्वभरि । ब्रह्माण्डभरि ।
कति चोरिरहनु उज्यालो
एक्लै मैले मात्र
स्वर्गबाट घरि-घरि ।

Promethean Sigh

Pity my arms they have turned to logs
from hauling light.
And still this thick, interminable
darkness of the world.

In the shadowless night's fort
if I too could hang my exhaustion
and nod off for a bit. How long
must I stare (for generations on end?)
wide-eyed in the crucible of sleep.

Let the eyes of the whole universe
be peeled open.
How long
should I alone
steal light from the heavens.

पीडाको अन्तिम कविता

मैले शब्दमा शब्दकै
पीडा खोजिरहेको छु । मेरो
पीडा छैन त्यहाँ । त्यहाँ
छैन । शब्दमा छैन सामर्थ्य
मेरो पीडा वहन गर्ने । मेरो
दुःख हर्ने ।

मेरो कण्ठका गीत
अनि यी मेरा कविता :
कतै शब्दको अर्चनाले पूजित दुषित कुन्ती,
कतै शब्दको प्रहारले कलंकित साध्वी सीता ।

ढुंगा पनि त शब्द हो । कति कठोर
हुन्छ त्यो । काँच पनि त शब्द हो । कति कम्जोर
हुन्छ त्यो । शब्दको एउटा कठोर ढुंगाको प्रहारले
शब्दकै एउटा कम्जोर काँच, सजिलै चर्काउन
सकिन्छ । कति बलिष्ट हुन्छ शब्दको सत्ता
फेरि कति निर्बल पनि ।

पीडाको गहनतामा शब्द पुग्दैनन्
पुग्छ केवल उच्छ्वास ।
उच्छ्वास : केवल चीसा-ताता श्वास
जो निःशब्द हुन्छन् ।

शब्द पुग्दैनन् पीडाको गहनतामा
पुग्छ केवल उच्छ्वास ।

Final Poem about Pain

I'm searching in a word the word's
agony. You won't
find my pain there. No.
The word cannot
ferry my pain, seize
my agony.

My full-throated song,
my poem:
in a word of adoration, wicked Kunti is worshipped,
in a word of assault, virtuous Sita condemned.

'Stone' too is a word. How
rigid it sounds. 'Glass' is a word also. How
fragile. A word's stone shatters
a word's fragile glass.
How formidable: word's sovereignty,
then again how powerless.

A word cannot travel to the depths of pain.
Only a sigh touches down there.
A sigh: lukewarm breath
          without speech.

The unknown depths of pain are a mystery to the word.
Only a sigh ever touches down.

मर्फिन : तृप्ति

ऐले रागले भरिएको छ मन
हाम्रो । झनझनाइरहेको छ कुनै रेल हिंडिसकेको
लीक झैं यो शरीर ।

कुटिम्रा र फलेदोका रूख तल
हामी थियौं कहिल्यै । अहिले छैनौं ।
तिमी त्यहाँ एक्लै पुगेर आयौ जुरेली झैं ।
मलाई यहाँ रूख हुन मन लागेको थियो । तिमीलाई
बास दिने रूख ।

अहिले मेरा दुवै हात शून्य छन् । रित्ता छन्
मस्तिष्कका अनेक दराजहरू । दराजहरूमा मर्फिनी
गन्ध कतै वर्तमान छ भित्र-भित्र । त्यहाँ
चल्मलाउँछन् कसैका औंला, सुम्सुम्याइँमा
माछा झैं ।

अहिले बल्ल लाग्दै छ–
मेरो मनको गमलामा कुनै बोट छ । अनि
त्यस बोटमा फूल छ तृप्ति-बोधको ।
मलाई कतै तिर्खा छैन ।

Morphine: Contentment

Now our hearts are full
of desire. Like a track reverberating
long after a train passes, our bodies.

Beneath the coral trees
we were, for a while. Now we aren't there.
You ventured alone and returned like the robin.
I wanted to be a tree right here. A tree
to offer you refuge.

My two hands return to nought. Vacant,
the many cabinets of my mind. Their insides
redolent with morphine. There—
someone's fingers stir and slither
like a fish.

Only now can I feel
a tree in the bed of my heart.
In that tree, flowers of contentment.
No drought inside me now.

अभीष्ट

बतासको भरमा उभिने
धूलोको शरीर, लडिहालेको देखेको छु
एक्कै छिनमा ।

त्यसैले. अरूको आश्रय होइन
मलाई आफ्नै आधार प्रिय छ ।

Intended

Propped up by a gust of wind
I have seen a body of dust
crumble in a second.

I don't need another's refuge.
The ground beneath is enough for me.

आत्म-पक्ष

मलाई केही भन्नु छैन ।

मैले जे-जति भन्नु थियो त्यो
नदीले नै भनिदियो । मेरो
मनको नदी । जसको तलमा
विचारका अनेक माछा छन्
संवेदनशील । पर्दैनन् तिम्रो प्रलोभनको
बल्छीमा यी माछा । [व्यर्थ अनि अनिर्भर
तिमीले अमोघ चिताएका शब्द-शर ।]

मलाई केही भन्नु छैन । मैले
जे-जति भन्नु थियो त्यो
नदीले नै भनिदियो
मेरो मनको नदी ।

तिमीले बुझ्नेनौ बन्धु मनको भाषा ।
केही पनि त बुझ्नेनौ बन्धु !

Soulward

I have nothing to say.

Whatever I had to say
was uttered by the river. River
of my heart. In the depths of which
swim my thoughts' myriad fish,
so tenderly. They won't be lured
by your bait. (Futile, imprecise
your word-arrows.)

I have nothing to say. Whatever
I had to say
was said by the river.
My heart's river.

Comrade, you did not understand the heart's language.
Not a single thing you've understood.

मनलाई लिएर : एउटा कविता

कस्सिएको वीणाको तार झैं
सचेत एउटा मन छ
मसित । तिमीले छोई मात्र दिए हुन्छ
औंलाले – चाल पाइहाल्छ । घोंच्नु पर्दैन ।
दु:खले टन्टनाइरहेकै हुन्छ
छोए बजिदिन्छ ।

केही लाखापाखा भएका सपनाहरू बटुलेर
आकाश तल उभिन खोज्दै छु लोलाएका खुट्टाले
टेकेर । लेखाजोखा नभएका अपाहिज इच्छाहरूले
आई / मेरा कुजा सपनाहरूलाई बैसाखी टेकाउँछन् ।
शायद यही थलोबाट थालेको छु बाँच्न मैले
यदि जिन्दगी यही हो भने ।

हिनामिना भएर छरपस्टिएका स्मृतिलाई
उन्न सकिने भए कुनै धागोमा / शायद
मैले गुमाएका सब्बै दिनहरू मसँगै हुने थिए
आज । साल बनको बतास, गुलाफ-गुलाफ प्रहर,
मेघ-मेघ एकान्त – मैले मनग्गे भोगेको छु ।
घरिघरि मलाई यिनको खाँचो पर्ने थिएन ।
जिन्दगी यसै खँदिलो हुने थियो सपनाबिना पनि ।

कस्सिएको वीणाको तार झैं
सचेत एउटा मन छ
मसित ।

Concerning the Heart

Strung taut like a harp string,
animate, I have one
heart. You only have to touch
with your finger—to feel it. No need to prod.
Forever throbbing in pain
it will sing at your touch.

Shoring littered dreams
I'm trying to stand under the sky on legs
that have fallen asleep. My misfired,
infirm desires / give crutches to my dreams.
Perhaps from this place I have begun
to live, if this is living.

Misplaced and scattered memories,
if only I could weave a bright thread through them /
perhaps the days I have lost would be here
still. Wind through the sal trees, rose-hued evenings,
fog-draped solitude—I once had my fill of these.
Oh to never look back.
My life would've been worthy even without them.

Strung taut like a harp string,
animate, I have one
heart.

इतिहास-पुरूष

उनीहरू जब बोल्छन्
उनीहरूको मुखुन्डो मात्र बोल्छ
मुख बोल्दैन ।
उनीहरू जब हिंड्छन्
उनीहरूको जुत्ता मात्र चल्छ
पैतला चल्दैन ।
त्यसैले हो क्या'र
उनीहरूको बोली समाचार बन्छ
लाखौं बिक्छ ।
उनीहरूको जुत्ता
म्यूजियमको शोभा बन्छ
युगौं टिक्छ ।

History-Men

When they talk
only their skulls speak
not their lips.
When they walk
only their shoes move
not their feet.
Perhaps that is why
their talk becomes news,
sells millions.
Their shoes
grace museums,
last aeons.

पूर्ववत्

आऊ, हामीहरू त्यहाँ जाऊँ
जहाँ हामीभित्र खप्टिएका मान्छेहरू दङ्ग परून्
आफ्नै छायाँ देखेर...

Antecedence

Come, let us go to that place
where all the people eclipsed beneath ourselves are astounded
by their own shadows.

मुटु : केक्टस

शरीरको मरूभूमिमा उम्रिन्छ
एउटा बोट केक्टसको ।
कठोरता र शुष्कतासित संघर्ष गर्न ।
हामीले भूल गरिरहेका छौं सधैं
त्यसलाई 'मुटु' भनेर ।

अरूको होस् न होस्
स्वीकार्छु म
मेरो मुटु केक्टस हो ।

Cactus

In the desert of the body
grows a cactus.
To prepare oneself against hardness and sterility.
We are mistaken
trying to pass it for a heart.

I don't know about everyone else
but I'll say this—
My heart is a cactus.

परेवा : सेता-काला

(कवि हरिभक्त कटुवाललाई समर्पित)

उमेर बिसाऊँ-बिसाऊँ झैं लाग्छ
यी नीला शिरीषका फूलहरूमा । कसले पो
बुझेको छ र समयको लहड । अर्को छिनमै
कुन कोल्टे बसिदिने हो ।

आँखाहरूलाई टेकाउँदा-टेकाउँदै
जिन्दगी थेग्ने कुनै सबल धारणाको ढुङ्गामा
चिप्लिएर गए लेउमा खुट्टा झैं । मनलाई
छोप्दा-छोप्दै, बाँद्धा-बाँद्धै इच्छाहरूले
फुत्किदियो खुकुलो सुर्के गाँठो झैं ।

चिनाउँदा-चिनाउँदै रहरलाई मन
र मनलाई रहर । धपाउँदा-धपाउँदै आँखाअघिबाट
उमेरका सेता-काला परेवा । म सक्किएँ ।
तर न मनले रहर चिन्यो । न रहले बुझिदियो मन ।

अझ पनि लाग्दै छ-
उमेर बिसाऊँ एक्कै छिनलाई भए पनि
यी नीला शिरीषका फूलहरूमा ।
बैंसले नेटो काटेर के भयो
मन त साबिकै छ !

Pigeons: White, Black

(For poet Haribhakta Katuwal)

A wish to rest my age among these blue
mimosa blooms. Who has known
the vagaries of time. The next moment
someone might topple over and croak.

While trying to rest my eyes on the ground
life slipped on wisdom's wet rock
like someone's feet on algae. Trying
to cover the heart, trying to bind my desires together
even as they come undone like a weak knot.

Trying to acquaint desire to heart
and heart to desire. Trying to drive from my eyes
the white and black pigeons of age. I've come to an end.
Neither heart understood desire. Nor desire understood heart.

Even so, this wish—
to rest my age for a while
among these blue mimosa blooms.
So what if age has crossed lines of sight,
the heart precedes it!

एउटा एलिजी

(कवि भैरव अर्याललाई समर्पित संवेदना)

समकालीन तटस्थता भिरेको मेरो भीरू मुटु
रन्थनिएको छ मित्र । तिम्रो मृत्युको साक्षी
फलाक्ने बाग्मतीको संग्लो पानी
फेरि धमिलिन थालेको छ ।

गति फेर्न नसकेको बूढो जर्जर इतिहास
अजिंगरको फ्याँकिएको भारी जीउ जस्तै
आफ्नै निम्ति समस्या भइदिएको बेला
तिमी आत्तियौ मित्र । भोलिको निश्चित उज्यालोमा
हामीसितै रमाउने मन एउटा तिमीले
निर्जीव तुल्यायौ हतारमा ।

आवेशमा निर्णय हुँदैन मित्र,
तिमीले इतिहास बिर्सेको बेला
हामीले एउटा सम्भावना गुमायौं ।

उत्कण्ठित उखरमाउलो स्रष्टाको जीवनमा
कहाँ हुँदैन र आकाश जस्तै ?
बाग्मती छिया-छिया भइन्होला
तिम्रो भोग लिंदा ।

An Elegy for a Poet

(In Memoriam: Bhairav Aryal)

My timid, indifferent heart
is restless today, friend. The clear Bagmati
river that cried witness to your death
is beginning to cloud again.

When history, decrepit and frail, couldn't change
its course, like a python's belly splayed
heavy, became its own impediment,
you panicked, friend. Your heart,
which in tomorrow's certain light would've laughed among us,
you pronounced it lifeless in haste.

Passion muddles judgement, friend
when you forgot history for a moment
we were robbed of possibility.

This life forged out of chaos & passion—
How will it not be like the sky?
Bagmati must've torn herself to shreds
when she took your offering in her belly.

तिम्रो करूण बिदामा
हाम्रा ओठ चुप्प लागेका छन् । तर तिम्रो
अयाचित मृत्युले झन् खँदिलो बनेका
हाम्रा संकल्पहरू बेहोश छैनन् ।

यस बेला, तिनै उद्विग्न संकल्पहरू
तिम्रा निम्ति प्रार्थना बनून् ।

Your merciful exit
has muted our lips. Yet, our resolution
bolstered by your sudden death
isn't dormant.

At this time, may these mournful resolutions
be prayers for you.

क्रान्तिको मानचित्र

जाँगर छैन मसित
पीरसित जिस्कने । मलाई
गाउन देऊ हुन्डरीको भाका हालेर
शोषित मान्छेको छातीमा उकुसमुकुसिएका
हाहाकारका गीतहरू ।

उखेल्नेछु यी चट्टान माटोको मस्तिष्कबाट ।
अनि त्यसलाई टेको दिने ढुंगाहरू
खोस्रेर मिल्क्याइदिनेछु । मैले इतिहासलाई
वचन दिइसकेको छु-
यस चट्टानले ओगटेको यो माटोमा
फूलबारी हुनेछ रमाइलो ।

रगतको बली खाई-खाई ढाडिएका
यी चट्टान जो देउता झैं पुजाउँछन्
आफैलाई / म यिनलाई उप्क्याएर
फ्याँकिछोड्ने छु । म हिमालको छोरो,
ब्रह्मपुत्रको पानी अञ्जुलीमा लिएर
किरिया खाँदै छु अहिले ।

मैले यो माटोको दिन फेर्ने बिंडा उठाएको छु
काँधमा आफ्नो । मैले मेरा यी दुई सबल
पाखुरामा बोकेको छु क्रान्तिको मानचित्र ।

Map of a Revolution

I'm not eager to make light
of grief. Let me sing
to the metre of the hurricane
the songs of lamentation stifled
in the chest of a Dalit man.

I'll tear this rock from the soil's sensorium.
I'll scratch loose the stones at its base
and fling them. I have given
my word to history—
Where the rock has usurped this soil
there shall be a garden.

Fattened on sacrificial blood
these rocks that want to be worshipped
like gods / I will peel
and cast them off. Son of mountain, I
pour the waters of the Brahmaputra in offering
and make an oath.

I have taken the ancient task of the soil's transformation
upon my shoulders. I have carried on my two arms
the map of a revolution.

दरिद्र

गाली र गोलीका माझबाट
भिक्षा र झोलीका माझबाट
भीड र नाराका माझबाट
मुस्कान र दाह्राका माझबाट
ऊ यौटा कम्जोर शब्द हो त्यसैले
सबथोक सहन्छ। नुघ्छ। खुम्चिन्छ।
आँखा नजुझाई
ठूल्ठूला शब्दहरूको छेउ लागी सहजै गुज्रिन्छ।

चिनामा उसको नाम लेखिएको रहेछ
'दरिद्र'।

ऊ त्यस्तो बारूद हो, साथी हो !
भोकले ओस्सिन्छ
चोटले ओस्सिन्छ
अपसोचले ओस्सिन्छ
खोस्सिन्छ ओस्सिन्छ
दोषिन्छ ओस्सिन्छ
होच्चिन्छ ओस्सिन्छ
चिमोटिन्छ ओस्सिन्छ

हेप्पिदा-हेप्पिदै
विद्रोहले तताउँछ
र सबै सखाप पार्ने गरी
ऊ एक्कासी पड्किन्छ।

ऊ त्यस्तो बारूद हो, साथी हो !

Poor

Between the berating and the bullet
Between the alms and the begging bowl
Between the mob and the slogan
Between the smile and the fangs
He is one weak word
so he endures. Bows. Bends.
Without looking them in the eyes
he skirts around the big-big words.

In his horoscope the name seems to be already written:
'Poor'.

He is that kind of gunpowder, comrades.
Dampened by hunger
dimmed by sorrow
torn, muffled.
blamed, dulled
diminished, blunted.
wrenched, stifled.

Oppressed day after day
a revolt begins to heat in him
then one day annihilating everything around him
he explodes.

He is that kind of gunpowder, comrades.

कविताको नायक : त्यो सैनिक

साङ्लो छिनालेर दगुर्न खोज्छन्
उसभित्रका असंख्य उन्मत्त घोडाहरू
यौवनका। उसको हाड-हाडमा भने
उसले अनुभव गर्छ सधैं
पुसको ठिही।

एउटा हात उसले गुमाएको छ। बारूदको
गन्धमा उसले फेरि अनुभव गर्छ
त्यो हात। सल्बलाइरहने ती औंलाहरू,
अनि अस्पतालको एकान्तमा / हात सँगसँगै
एउटा खुट्टाबाट पनि वञ्चित हुनुको
ऐनेस्थेसिया गन्धमा डुबेको बोध।

अबउसो न बन्दूक उठाउन सक्ने छ
उसले। न झण्डा। न मुटुभरि
बोक्न सक्ने छ कसैको छिर्केमिर्के
आश्वासन। मनमा कतै भित्रिँदै जाने
झिनो पगध्वनि।

अपाहिजत्वबाट जोगयाउन आफ्नो देश
ऊ अपाहिज भयो। अपाहिज भए
उसका सपनाहरू। बैसाखीमा बुई चढ्न
वाध्य छन / अब उसका युवा इच्छाहरू।

न मनको ओढारमा टहटह जून लाग्ने छ
अब / न सुनिने छ त्यो एकान्तको मौनता
भत्काउँदै / कसैको पगध्वनि।

This Poem's Hero: That Soldier

They want to break the fetters and escape—
the lusty horses of his youth
cooped up inside him. But in the marrow
of his bones he feels
the long winter's chill.

He has lost a limb. In a whiff of gunpowder
stirs the ghost of his missing
hand. His serpentine fingers.
In the hospital's solitude / redolent with anaesthesia
a sudden intimation of being robbed
of a leg too.

He can neither pick up a rifle
nor a flag now. Or bear
in his heart someone else's mottled
pledge. The sound of weak footsteps
paddles into his heart.

To save his country from losing an arm
he crippled himself. Crippled
his dreams. All his tender desires
forced to piggyback on a crutch.

Neither will the moon shine blindingly
inside the den of his heart now / nor the sound
of someone's footsteps / break its solitary quiet.

केही फुटकर टुक्राहरू

१. रूपान्तर

दिन आउँछ
कोपिलामा फूल आए झैं,
सुइरोमा पात आए झैं ।

दिन जान्छ
जसरी खरानीमा अङ्गार जान्छ,
मेघमा सागर जान्छ ।

२. अरू कोई त्यो

म सँग-सँगै हिंड्छ
अरू कोई त्यो
मेरो सहयात्री ।
म गौंडो उक्लिरहन्छु
ऊ झर्छ । म सधैं घसारिइरहन्छु
बाँचाइको सीमानातिर
ऊ मर्छ ।

कठै बिचरा त्यो, मेरो आयु ।

Fragments

1. Transformation

Day comes
like a flower on a bud,
like a leaf on a branch.

Day goes
like ember in ashes,
like the sea to the clouds.

2. The Other

There's someone else
that walks beside me
a fellow traveller.
I keep scaling the narrow pass
he falls. I keep dragging myself
to the borders of living
he dies.

Pity, the poor fool, my age.

३. तिमी

तिमी निविड यन्त्रणा माझको प्रेरणा हौ ।
युद्धको विभीषिका माझ पिल्सिएकाहरूले
एक्कासि सुन्न पाएको शान्तिको घोषणा हौ ।

४. तिमी

तिमी पीडा झैं गहन छ्यौ ।
फेरि पनि चिहान झैं मौन छ्यौ ।

3. You

In the middle of bleak affliction you are encouragement.
In the midst of the battlefield's terror
the sudden call for peace heard by the lacerated.

4. You

Like grief you are impenetrable.
Then again, like a grave you are silent.

Acknowledgements

My sincere thanks to the editors and staff of the following publications for featuring work from the book, sometimes in earlier versions:

The Progressive: 'Metamorphosis' (as 'Renewal'); 'Relative'
Poetry London: 'Headland—2'
Words Without Borders: 'Of Some Unidentified Village, Nayantara Barua'
Circumference: 'Monologue'; 'Labour-Song'; 'Aside'
South Parade: 'Same City, Same River'; 'City'; 'River Raga—1, 2'; 'Headland—1'
The Bombay Literary Magazine: 'On Descending a Fog-Rimmed Mountain'; 'Song of the Five Elements'; 'Spell'
Poet Tree: 'Incongruity'
Modern Poetry in Translation: 'Map of a Revolution'; 'Poor'; 'My Poems'

In gratitude: Avinash Shrestha, for trusting my hand with these poems and for being ever so patient with me over the years. Anita Tandukar, for her selfless and stellar work on the transcription of the Nepali poems. Manjushree Thapa, for the initial introduction to the author. Brooks Haxton, whose introductory translation workshop during my MFA at Syracuse University was instrumental in kick-starting this project. Roberto Tejada and Jamie Ferguson, whose translation seminars and graduate workshops I took towards a Certificate in Translation Studies during my PhD at University of Houston. Their deep engagement with the craft and the history of translation further refined my project and became a model for my work as an emerging translator. The jury of the PEN/Heim Translation Grant for the early recognition of the project. The Institute for World Literature (IWL) conference, 2021, where I had the opportunity to take a seminar with Lawrence Venuti. Ibrahim Badshah, with whom I've had countless fruitful conversations about translation over biryani and Mehdi Hassan in Houston. Vivek Narayanan, from whom I've learned so much over the years in our discussions about translation and poetry. Victor Hernandez, whose support for the project has been constant and enthusiastic as ever. My partner, Kaitlin Rizzo, my in-house editor and fashion consultant extraordinaire, for all her enthusiasm and belief in my writing. My brother, Ankeet Poudel, and sister-in-law, Sajina G.C., for their support and inputs early on. My parents, my family, especially my grandmother Geeta Chhetri to whom this book is dedicated. Finally, I couldn't have asked for a better editor than Rahul Soni, an extraordinary translator himself, to ferry this project out into the world.

—Rohan Chhetri

About the Author

About the Author

Born on 14 May 1955 in Guwahati, India, **Avinash Shrestha** went to Nepal for postgraduate studies in 1984, and after a brief return to India moved to Kathmandu permanently in 1990. Heavily influenced by the regional poetry movements in India, Shrestha had already written a book of poems in Assamese and two volumes of his Nepali poetry had been published in Assam. His first published collection of poetry in Nepali, *Samvedna, O Samvedna!* (1981) established his foothold in the Nepali literary map. His third book, and his first to be published in Nepal, *Anubhuti Yatrama*, came out in 1990. His most recent full-length collection, *Karodoun Suryaharuko Andhakar* was published in 2003. A prolific and versatile writer and editor in Nepal with numerous feature film and television scripts, songs and plays to his credit, Shrestha's literary works have been awarded the prestigious Mainali Katha Puraskar, the Nepal Motion Picture Award, the Dhaulagiri Sahitya Puraskar (for the poetry collection *Anubhuti Yatrama*), and the Yuva Barsha Moti Puraskar among others. In June 2022 he was awarded the prestigious Gopal Prasad Rimal Smriti Samman for his contribution to contemporary Nepali literature. He was the chief editor of the literary magazine *Garima,* and is the founder and editor emeritus of the Royal Nepal Academy's literary magazine, *Samakalin Sahitya*.

About the Translator

Rohan Chhetri is the author of *Slow Startle*, and *Lost, Hurt, or in Transit Beautiful*, which was awarded the Kundiman Poetry Prize. He has also co-edited *Shreela Ray: On the Life and Work of an American Master*. His poems and translations have appeared in *The Paris Review, Poetry London,* the Academy of American Poets' *Poem-a-Day,* and *Words Without Borders*, among others, and in numerous anthologies including *The Forward Book of Poetry 2023* and *The Bloomsbury Anthology of Great Indian Poems*. His poems have been translated into Turkish, Greek and French.